P9-ELI-346

Joan Halifax

shaman

The wounded healer

with 131 illustrations, 16 in colour

Thames and Hudson

All Shamans know that Death furnishes all with Life

Northern Cheyenne Medicine Chief, Hyemeyohsts Storm

This book is a Giveaway
to All My Relations

The following people, among many others, have
been of great assistance with this book. I express
my deepest gratitude to: John Barazzuol, Richard
Barazzuol, Jean Butler, Joseph Campbell, Ed
Canda, Leonard Crow Dog, Richard Erdoes, Louis
Faron, Peter Furst, Robert Gardner, Ksan Jones,
Stephanie Leonard, Janet Mackenzie, Matsuwa,
Daniel Melnick, Peter Melnick, Barbara Myerhoff,
Juan Negrin, Lita O'Dell, Robert Ott, Prem Das, Jill
Purce, Gerardo Reichel-Dolmatoff, Ruturi,
Richard Evans Schultes, Douglas Sharon,
Hyemeyohsts Storm, Mrs T. G. H. Strehlow, Sun
Bear and Wabun, Harley Swiftdeer, R. Gordon
Wasson, Paula White.

JH, Mt Shasta, July 1981

ART AND IMAGINATION
General Editor: Jill Purce

Any copy of this book issued by the publisher as a
paperback is sold subject to the condition that it
shall not by way of trade or otherwise be lent,
resold, hired out or otherwise circulated without
the publisher's prior consent in any form of binding
or cover other than that in which it is published
and without a similar condition including these
words being imposed on a subsequent purchaser.

First published in Great Britain in 1982
Reprinted 1988

© 1982 Thames and Hudson Ltd, London

All Rights Reserved. No part of this publication may
be reproduced or transmitted in any form or by
any means, electronic or mechanical, including
photocopy, recording or any other information
storage and retrieval system, without prior
permission in writing from the publisher.

Printed and bound in Singapore by
C.S. Graphics Pte Ltd.

Contents

The wounded healer

Plates   33

Themes   65

Sources and acknowledgments   96

The wounded healer

The lifeway of the shaman is nearly as old as human consciousness itself, predating the earliest recorded civilizations by thousands of years. Through the ages, the practice of shamanism has remained vital, adapting itself to the ways of all the world's cultures. Today the role of shaman takes many forms – healer, ceremonialist, judge, sacred politician, and artist, to name a few. The shaman lies at the very heart of some cultures, while living in the shadowy fringe of others. Nevertheless, a common thread seems to connect all shamans across the planet. An awakening to other orders of reality, the experience of ecstasy, and an opening up of visionary realms form the essence of the shamanic mission.

In no way does this volume offer a comprehensive or detailed view of shamanism. Rather it offers a summary of various forms of shamanism, and a generalized model based on the psychosymbolic structures emerging from the ground of many shamanic cultures. I have organized the book around the theme of voyage, focusing on the inner journey shamans take during a life crisis and the ways in which they order the chaos and confusion of the voyage into Cosmos. The extraordinary consistency of the shamanic complex emerges in the study of this ordering process. That this commonality cuts across seemingly irreconcilable ethnic and cultural lines attests to the mystery and power lying at the source of myth, the human psyche.

One stylistic note seems unavoidable. Although the practice of shamanism has greatly diminished over the past century with the introduction of technology to many protohistorical cultures, the 'ethnographic present' is used in this book in keeping with current anthropological style.

Patterns of the mythic imagination

Shamanic knowledge is remarkably consistent across the planet. In spite of cultural diversity and the migration and diffusion of peoples across the earth, the basic themes related to the art and practice of shamanism form a coherent complex. Cultural variations do exist – and yet, when examining the field, there are superficial features as well as deeper structures which appear to be constant.

This Eskimo carving, of a shaman harpooning himself, captures the essence of the shaman's submission to a higher order of knowing. (Carving in grey stone, ivory and bone by EMIK, from Payne Bay, 1949.)

Shamanism's origins in the Palaeolithic period inevitably link it with the animal world of the hunt. The shaman became identified metaphysically with the untamed creatures which provided food, clothing, and even shelter. An Iglulik Eskimo elucidated this concept to the Arctic explorer

A spirit of the sea accompanied by a gull seems to be bestowing a boon. The singular vitality that characterizes the art of shamanic cultures points to the belief in a pervasive force or presence in nature that can be channelled by seers and wizards in the special circumstances of shamanic rapture. (Stonecut print by Kenojuak, Eskimo, Cape Dorset, 1963.)

The Indians from the Vaupés area of Colombia, according to anthropologist Gerardo Reichel-Dolmatoff, use plant hallucinogens in order to establish direct contact with the supernatural realm. The visionary plants themselves are believed to be the residence of spirit powers. The Desana of the Vaupés often paint the walls of their communal houses (malocas) with spirit images that they have seen in their hallucinogenic trances. (Drawing, after Reichel-Dolmatoff, The Shaman and the Jaguar, of spirit image from Bará maloca, Pira-paraná.)

1 Rasmussen, *Intellectual Culture of the Iglulik Eskimos*, 55–6.

2 Eliade, *Shamanism*, 504.

3 Halifax, *Shamanic Voices*.

Knud Rasmussen: 'The greatest peril of life lies in the fact that human food consists entirely of souls. All the creatures that we have to kill and eat, all those that we have to strike down and destroy to make clothes for ourselves, have souls, souls that do not perish with the body and which must therefore be (pacified) lest they should revenge themselves on us for taking away their bodies.'[1]

Through this cathexis to the realm of creatures, the Palaeolithic shaman sought to control directly the animals of the hunt and to become the master of wild game and a summoner of beasts. Animal sacrifice, bird shaman staffs, animal familiars and the animal costumes of lion, bull, bear, and stag all played a part in the Palaeolithic shamanic complex. In the Franco-Cantabrian cave of Les Trois Frères, for example, one finds the 15,000-year-old image of the Sorcerer dancing above a gambolling tangle of beasts, in the centre of which a shaman dressed as a bison dances and plays a hunting-bow (see pp. 54–5). Dance and trance were surely central to early shamanism, as they are to the continuing practice of this art of ecstasy.

The experience of ecstasy, states Mircea Eliade, is a timeless 'primary phenomenon'.[2] Psychological experiences of rapture, he continues, are fundamental to the human condition, and hence known to the whole of archaic humanity. The evaluation of these visionary experiences often results in local, culture-bound interpretations. However, narratives of contemporary shamans testify to the uniformity of the symbolic content of these raptures.[3] From Lapland to Patagonia, from the Palaeolithic to today, the archetypes activated during shamanic ordeals and exaltations are astonishingly similar.

As we review the visions of shamans from archaic times to the very present, the theme of the great quest undertaken during states of painful rapture weaves across the loom of many cultures. It is this metaphysical voyage that is to be explored here.

The steps of the journey of shamanic initiation seem to have a patterned course. The call to power necessitates a separation from the mundane world: the neophyte turns away from the secular life, either voluntarily, ritually, or spontaneously through sickness, and turns inward towards the unknown, the *mysterium*. This change of direction can be accomplished only through what Carl Jung has referred to as 'an obedience to awareness'. Only through the development of discipline will the shaman's habitual ways of seeing and behaving dissolve, and the visionary realms open. Thus, the initial call to power takes the shaman to the realm of chaos, the *limen*, where power exists in a free and untransformed state.

From every point of view, the shaman awakens psychologically in the process of mystical realizations attained in trance. The mythologies of shamanic peoples, symbolic features of the shamanic complex, and curing techniques are all based on the ecstatic experience. The deepest structures within the psyche are found in the themes of descent to the Realm of Death, confrontations with demonic forces, dismemberment, trial by fire, communion with the world of spirits and creatures, assimilation of the elemental forces, ascension via the World Tree and/or the Cosmic Bird, realization of a solar identity, and return to the Middle World, the world of human affairs. The shaman, however, has a social rather than a personal reason for opening the psyche as he or she is concerned with the community and its well-being; sacred action, then, is directed towards the creation of order out of chaos.

Thus, through a profound process of psychic turbulence and combustion, the images of the mythic imagination are awakened. These transpersonal and transcultural realizations are known even in modern psychiatry, where their evaluation is generally of a pathological nature. However, the insights of psychiatrist John Weir Perry into the psychosymbolic processes of individuals diagnosed as schizophrenic give us important clues about the archetypal nature of the shamanic complex.[4] Dr Perry elaborates ten features that characterize the reorganization of the Self. (1) Psychic, cosmic, and personal geography are focused on a *centre*. (2) *Death* occurs in the process of dismemberment and sacrifice; the person is tortured, chopped up, and his or her bones are rearranged; one can also be dead and talk with presences of the spirit world. (3) There is a *return* to an earlier time, to Paradise, or to the womb; the theme of regression can also be reflected in the individual manifesting the behaviour of an infant. (4) There arises a *cosmic conflict* between forces of Good and Evil, or other pairs of opposites. (5) There is a feeling of being overwhelmed by the opposite sex; the *threat of the opposite* can also manifest in terms of a positive identification with one's opposite. (6) The transformation of the individual results in a mystical *apotheosis* where the experiencer becomes identified with a cosmic or royal personage. (7) The person enters into a *sacred marriage*, a coming together of the pairs of opposites. (8) A *new birth* is part of rebirth fantasies and experiences. (9) A new age or the beginning of a *new society* is anticipated. (10) The balance of all elements results in the *quadrated world*, a four-fold structure of equilibrium and depth.

The Renewal of the Self, as Dr Perry describes this process, has striking parallels in the shamanic complex. Each feature has its counterpart in the psychosymbolism and mythos of the protohistorical world. It is at the Centre of the Cosmos that the shaman is to be found, where the three worlds – Underworld, Middle World and Sky Realm – are encountered. The Centre, Axis Mundi, or *Nieríka* is the path, passage, or gateway to the Realm of Death, where the shaman confronts demonic forces that dismember. This confrontation takes place in the cosmic womb of the Earth Mother, in the bowels of the Underworld, in the primordial beginning, before Time. The battle between the shaman and elemental forces can also be manifested in the inchoate fear of the power of the contrary, the Siberian shaman's terrified resistance against androgynization, for example. After surrender, apotheosis is attained by means of a mystical identification with fire. The sacred marriage with the untamed spirit of the opposite sex brings together the pairs of opposites. As a consequence, a birth and rebirth can occur in the highest branches of the World Tree. The theme of new birth has its

4 Perry, *The Far Side of Madness.*

7

parallel in an earlier stage, that of regression and return, as does the sacred marriage with its counterpart in the struggle against being consumed or devoured by the opposite sex. As the shaman is reborn, so is the society reborn, for the shaman manifests an image of a harmonious cosmos: the cosmic design is of an ordered universe where the four winds, four roads, or four directions are balanced in a world renewed.

This mystery is experienced by the shaman in visions, in dreams, in exalted raptures. As the California Pomo shaman, Essie Parrish, said of her journey, 'I don't have to go nowhere to see. Visions are everywhere.' And this was her revelatory journey:

It is a test you have to pass. Then you can learn to heal with the finger. I went through every test on the way, that's how come I'm a shaman. 'Be careful on the journey,' they said, 'the journey to heaven,' they warned me.

And so I went. Through rolling hills I walked. Mountains and valleys, and rolling hills, I walked and walked – you hear many things there in those rolling hills and valleys, and I walked and walked until I came to a foot bridge, and on the right side were a whole lot of people and they were naked and crying out, 'How'd you get over there, we want to get over there, too, but we're stuck here; please come over here and help us across, the water's too deep for us.' I didn't pay no attention, I just walked and walked, and then I heard an animal, sounded like a huge dog, and there was a huge dog and next to him a huge lady wearing blue clothes, and I decided I had to walk right through; I did and the dog only snarled at me. Never go back. I walked and walked and I came to only one tree, and I walked over to it and looked up at it and read the message. Go on, you're half way. From there I felt better, a little better.

And I walked and walked and walked and walked and I saw water, huge water – how to get through? I fear it's deep. Very blue water. But I have to go. Put out the first foot, then the left, never use the left hand, and I passed through. Went on and on and on, and I had to enter a place and there I had to look down: it was hot and there were people there and they looked tiny down there in that furnace running around and crying. I had to enter. You see, these tests are to teach my people how to live. Fire didn't burn me. And I walked and walked and walked and walked. On the way you're going to suffer. And I came to a four-way road like a cross. Which is the right way? I already knew East is the right way to go to heaven. North, South and West are dangerous. At this crossroad there was a place in the center. North you could see beautiful things of the Earth, hills and fields and flowers and everything beautiful and I felt like grabbing it but I turned away. South was dark, but there were sounds, monsters and huge animals. And I turned away and Eastward I walked and walked and walked and there were flowers, on both sides of the road; flowers and flowers and flowers out of this world.

And there is white light at the center, while you're walking. This is the complicated thing: my mind changes. We are the people on the Earth. We know sorrow and knowledge and faith and talent and everything. Now as I was walking there, some places I feel like talking and some places I feel like dancing, but I am leaving these behind for the next world.

Then when I entered into that place I knew; if you enter heaven you might have to work. This is what I saw in my vision. I don't have to go nowhere to see. Visions are everywhere.[5]

The net of power

For the shaman, all that exists in the revealed world has a living force within it. This life energy force, like the Polynesian *mana* or the Sioux *wakanda*, is conceived of as a divine force which permeates all. The knowledge that life is power is the realization of the shaman. Communion with the purveyors of power is the work of the shaman. Mastery of that power: this is the attainment of the shaman.

In the Siberian Chukchee shamanic view of the cosmos, for example, that power suffuses all things, and everything has an endless potential for transformation. One Chukchee shaman told the anthropologist Waldemar Bogoras,

> On the steep bank of a river, there exists life. A voice is there, and speaks aloud. I saw the 'master' of the voice and spoke with him. He subjugated himself to me and sacrificed to me. He came yesterday and answered my questions. The small gray bird with the blue breast comes to me and sings shaman songs in the hollow of the bough, calls her spirits, and practices shamanism. The woodpecker strikes his drum in the tree with his drumming nose. Under the axe, the tree trembles and wails as a drum under the baton. All these come at my call.[1]

As the same Chukchee shaman stated, 'All that exists lives.' The shaman personalizes all phenomena in the universe, endowing them with human qualities. The tree trembles beneath the axe. The drum wails under the baton. All things have emotions which are subject to influence. In a cosmos that is essentially as unpredictable as the human realm, the shaman's tapping into power allows for the possible reversal of death, the transformation of form, and the transcendence of time and space.

Many shamanic peoples who associate power with both will and sentience believe that any being with the capacity for awareness has the potential for exercising power. The net of power animates the cosmos. The shaman plays into that net and is able to go far beyond the normal boundaries of human action and interaction.

The Blessed Ones tap into the net of power. Many others do not. As Sioux medicine-man, Lame Deer, once said of power, one does not inherit it. One can work for it, fast for it, try to dream it up, and yet the power does not always come. Not everyone is ready to be the master of power.

The initial call to power takes the shaman to the realm of chaos, the *limen*, where the cosmos is disorderly, where power moves freely – untransformed. The beginning of mastery of that power can be ecstatic. The act of mastery, however, implies that balance and equilibrium have been achieved, creating a right presence of mind. Only the practice of power allows for its mastery; and only through time and experience is the potentially damaging power safely manifested.

Chinese Taoist talismans are a practical form of magic with shamanistic elements which assists the procurement of good fortune, the avoidance of misfortune, and communication with spirits. At the philosophical level, the talismans represent the beneficial harmonization of Yin *and* Yang *in the cosmos. This talisman of the Heavenly Messenger features a figure with coiled body representing the 28 Constellations to assist brightness, which is* Yang, *and with legs to walk on the earth (*Yin) *in a manner which makes possible the destruction of evil spirits. (From Legeza, Tao Magic.)*

5 *Alcheringa. Ethnopoetics.*

1 Bogoras, *The Chuckchee*, 281.

This is why the ordeals that shamans must endure before moving into their full vocation are so demanding. The intention of the individual for whom power has been awakened is the absolute precondition determining whether power is used for good or evil purposes. The abuse of power is all too common, and when the obstacles to power and knowledge are great, the attrition of unprepared and unworthy seekers keeps the profession in the ethical realm. This is not to say, however, that all shamans are paragons of virtue. As Mexican Huichol shaman Ramon Medina Silva once said, 'In this world, one does not lack a sharp thing to stick in the eye.' Yet the hardship of learning can function to eliminate the least virtuous and strengthen the less virtuous.

The realization of power occurs most frequently in the midst of an ordeal, a crisis involving an encounter with death. It comes suddenly, in an instant, and in many ways the descriptions by shamans of their confrontations with power are comparable to accounts by yogis of the awakening of kundalini and by Zen masters of their experiences of enlightenment. The entrance to the other world occurs through the action of total disruption. The neophyte surrenders into the realm of chaos, frequently making use of the experience of fear and dread to amplify the intensity of the situation.

Paradoxically, the shaman's mastery of chaos can take the form of a battle with disease-spirits that overwhelm the neophyte to the point of near-death. These horrific adversaries become tutors as the shaman learns the ways of the spirits that ravage and cause sickness. The neophyte Underworld-voyager learns the battlefield that he or she will enter on behalf of others in the future. Here, the shaman acquires direct knowledge from direct experience. From this can come the opening of compassion and the awakening of empathy in the healer.

An elder from San Juan Pueblo in the southwestern United States describes the process thus:

> What I am trying to say is hard to tell and hard to understand ... unless, unless ... you have been yourself at the edge of the Deep Canyon and have come back unharmed. Maybe it all depends on something within yourself – whether you are trying to see the Watersnake or the sacred Cornflower, whether you go out to meet death or to Seek Life. It is like this: as long as you stay within the realm of the great Cloudbeings, you may indeed walk at the very edge of the Deep Canyon and not be harmed. You will be protected by the rainbow and the great Ones. You will have no reason to worry and no reason to be sad. You may fight the witches, and if you can meet them with a heart which does not tremble, the fight will make you stronger. It will help you to attain your goal in life; it will give you strength to help others, to be loved and liked, and to seek Life.[2]

Nature-Kin and interspecies communication

For the shaman, although the universe is conceived of as powerful and uncertain, it is also a cosmos that is personalized. Rocks, plants, trees, bodies of water, two-legged and four-legged creatures, as well as those creatures

2 Laski, *Seeking Life*, 128–9.

who swim or crawl – all are animate, all have personal identities. The cosmos in its parts as well as in its totality has will, rationality, awareness, and feeling. In fact, the world of the human and the world of nature and spirit are essentially reflections of each other in the shaman's view of the cosmos.

All aspects of the shaman's universe interact to greater or lesser degrees with greater or lesser power. According to certain mythologies, during the Paradisical time before Time, the cosmos had total access to itself. There was one language for all creatures and elements, and humankind shared that language. With the passage of time, however, the conditions of Paradise diminished. Power was vitiated, and the bonds of kinship with all life were broken. Thus a separation came about. Although the common language was lost, all phenomena in the cosmos are still interrelated, and the action of the human elements profoundly affects the state of nature and spirit.

The shamanic world view acknowledges this kinship among all aspects of nature. The primordial ancestors are Grandfather Fire, Grandmother Growth, Our Mother the Sea and Springs, Father Sun, and Mother Earth. The ancestors can be conceived thus bonded as Nature-Kin. In spite of this kinship, the universe is perceived as fraught with peril. With the end of Paradise came the beginning of Time and Death. The channels of communication giving access to the non-human realms were mostly broken. Ceremony and sacrifice can be regarded as attempts to re-establish the mystical unity of Paradise. Ritual action seeks some measure of contact with and control over spirits and other forces generally inaccessible to the ordinary human being.

The following account by an Eskimo shaman is recorded by Rasmussen:

(There is) a power we call Sila, which is not to be explained in simple words. A great spirit, supporting the world and the weather and all life on earth, a spirit so mighty that (what he says) to mankind is not through common words, but by storm and snow and rain and the fury of the sea; all the forces of nature that men fear. But he has also another way of (communication): by sunlight and calm of the sea, and little children innocently at play, themselves understanding nothing. Children hear a soft and gentle voice, almost like that of a woman. It comes to them in a mysterious way, but so gently that they are not afraid, they only hear that some danger threatens. And the children mention it (casually) when they come home, and it is then the business of the (shaman) to take such measures as shall guard against the danger. When all is well, Sila sends no message to mankind, but withdraws into his own endless nothingness, apart. So he remains as long as men do not abuse life, but act with reverence toward their daily food. . . .

No one has seen Sila; his place of being is a mystery, in that he is at once among us and unspeakably far away.[1]

This special and sacred awareness of the universe is codified in song and chant, poetry and tale, carving and painting. This art is not art for art, rather it is art for survival, for it gives structure and coherence to the unfathomable and intangible. By 'making' that which is the unknown, the shaman attains some degree of control over the awesome forces of the *mysterium*.

This drawing from the fresco in the Palaeolithic cave of Lascaux, France, depicts a sacrifice of a bison bull and an entranced shaman with his bird staff below and to the left of him. The spirit of the shaman and the bison are both liberated – one through death, the other in trance. Thus communication is established between nature and culture, the raw and the cooked. The shaman's rapture is not only indicated by his posture of repose but also by his erect penis. The spirit of the shaman is self-fertilized in the experience of ecstasy.

1 Rasmussen, *Across Arctic America*, 385–6.

Magic and the supernatural are the means that the shaman uses to gain control over a cosmos of uncertainty. Natural and supernatural events commingle in the person of the shaman. Through the power and knowledge of the wizard, equilibrium between the indeterminate and the predictable can be achieved. Though the shaman-neophyte may at the onset challenge the elements and the ancestors, discipline and obedience to the higher natural order is the way to an alliance with the supernatural.

In the Southern California Chumash tale that follows, the neophyte is brought to this alliance through sickness, solitude, insistence, and surrender.

Long, long ago, there lived a consumptive whose name was Axiwalic. Although he took much medicine to cure himself of sickness, he never seemed to improve. After a time, he began to despair of ever recovering, so grave was his illness. This was curious since Axiwalic was a wizard and had mustered all of his power in many attempts to cure himself. Finally, Axiwalic decided that nothing more could be done, so he left his village in search of a place to die.

He went to the sea, where he began to walk along the edge of the shore. As night fell, he stopped to rest, and, as he was sitting there, waiting, he saw a remarkable thing. A light emerged from a rock in a nearby cliff; it moved about and then re-entered the rock. Axiwalic sat there wondering about this little light. Soon the light came out of its place again, and the sick man said to himself, 'I'll seize it; I'll capture it with my power.'

The light then drifted toward him, and he grabbed it with his wizardry as a moth is caught with a handkerchief. Now the little *pelepel* (the *pelepel* is like a youth but shines like a light) cried out, 'Let me go.' It wanted to be released so it could return home.

When Axiwalic heard this, he pleaded with the *pelepel* to let him accompany him to his home. But the *pelepel* told the ailing wizard that it would not be possible. 'You can't get through that small hole.'

Axiwalic would not hear of this. He insisted that he would not release the *pelepel* unless he took Axiwalic with him. A terrific argument ensued. Back and forth, back and forth went the heated discussion. But Axiwalic was not to be dissuaded. At last, the *pelepel* gave in and agreed to take the sick man through the tiny hole in the cliff.

And so the journey began. The two entered the hole, and Axiwalic found himself travelling down a long tunnel with the *pelepel*. At the end of the tunnel, they reached a great house where the little light, the *pelepel*, disappeared.

Axiwalic sat down and began to look about to find out where he was. He saw many animals there in that great house. An old deer lying motionless was nearby and so was a beaver with a cloud of hail around his head. And many deer and birds were there, and they did not speak to him.

Soon more animals came into the great house, all creatures who walk upon four legs — coyotes, bears, wildcats, and many more. And all of these four-legged creatures defecated upon him until he was completely covered with faeces. And still the creatures were silent as Axiwalic sat there quietly watching.

The old deer at last approached him and asked, 'Why are you here?' Axiwalic replied, 'I am a sick man; I cannot recover.'

Then the old deer told Axiwalic, 'We shall have a fiesta, and we will bathe you.'

So the four-legged creatures prepared everything they needed for the fiesta, and when it was over, they gathered to bathe him. When he was cleansed, he became well, and his appetite returned, and he began to eat.

Then the old deer who had cured him told Axiwalic, 'We are now going to return you to your world.'

And so Axiwalic was returned to his village. But this time they did not send him by way of the long tunnel. Rather he passed through a spring to the world of his people. When he entered the village, all recognized him and cried out joyfully, 'He whom we believed to be dead has returned cured.'

Then Axiwalic began to tell the people everything that had happened to him – the tiny light coming from the hole in the cliff, the tunnel, the great house filled with four-legged creatures who soiled him, the fiesta and bath, and the return through the spring. When he was finished with his story, he was amazed to learn that he had been gone for three long years, for he thought he had been away for only three days.[2]

Three days dead, three years dead, like the dark of the moon, is the pause between the personal past and a realized, transtemporal life. Dreams and visions, madness and sickness cause the loss of the neophyte's soul. The soul thus freed of the time-governed mortal body is open to instruction and ultimately transformation. The soul can see its counterparts in the non-material world of spirits. This is, in essence, the sign of the true shamanic vocation. To have contact with the dead, says Mircea Eliade, is to be dead oneself. In Siberia, Australia, and the Americas, the shaman must die in order to communicate with the souls in the Afterlife Realm. It is in this way that shamans are taught, for the dead know everything.[3] Thus the dead assist the shaman in also becoming dead – this in order that he or she may achieve the spirit state.

The communication with creatures and spirits, with those that are regarded as non-human, is effected in the shamanic seance; the sacred medium in trance is possessed by gods or spirits who use him or her as a means of divine transmission. The shaman is the channel for interspecies communication, and the spirits borrow or take over him or her for this purpose.

Among the Ainu of Hokkaido Japan, the great epics sung by the shamans are songs sung by gods to gods and ultimately to humans. The use of the first person in these narratives is an ancient means wherein the shaman speaks for the gods and the gods speak through the shaman.

The Ainu shaman (often a woman) is depicted in these great epics as being surrounded by her spirit-allies: 'Her visible companion spirits/flocked about her/darkly/like a bunch of bats/and her invisible companion spirits/twinkled/over her head/like stars flashing'.[4] According to Ainu scholar, Donald Philippi, Ainu poetry is essentially a process of self-revelation. During a performance, the shaman-reciter's identity is

2 After Blackburn (ed.), *December's Child*, 233–4.

3 Eliade, *Shamanism*, 84.

4 Philippi, *Songs of Gods, Songs of Humans*, 45.

The drum, the dance, and the shaman's mask all point to an unearthly transtemporal experience of ecstasy that opens communication with the supernatural. In this way the shaman stands outside what he or she is in ordinary life, to become a mediator between the untamed forces of nature and the human community. (Drawing after rock carving, Lake Onega region, USSR, c. 5000–1500 BC.)

5 Philippi, Songs of Gods, Songs of Humans, 59.

6 Bogoras, The Chuckchee, 416.

overwhelmed by the presence of the heroes and heroines, gods and spirits.

In the world-view of the Ainu shaman, all creatures and entities that are non-human are regarded as gods (kami) – that is, 'they are non-human beings with supernatural attributes who live in thoroughly anthropo-morphic fashion in their own god-worlds, where they are invisible to human eyes, but who also share a common territory with humans and pay frequent visits to the humans in disguise. Animals are such gods in disguise'.[5]

The world, then, for the Ainu, is a common territory inhabited by humans and gods, the gods being represented by nature. The human realm is totally dependent on the gods for survival. The relationship is one of interdependence between species. Only the shaman is able to behave as both a god and a human. The shaman then is an interspecies being, as well as a channel for the gods. He or she effects the interpenetration of diverse realms.

The connection between the human realm and the Nature-Kin is a continuum that is sought after by the shaman-neophyte. The shaman's ability to transform himself or herself into a spirit entity bespeaks the power that is realized in the process of metamorphosis from one state to another. This temporary loss of humanity on the shaman's part is a revolutionary phenomenon in the sense that the shaman regains human attributes when the trance-cycle is complete.

Among the Siberian Chukchee, those shamans who arrive at their vocation through personal inspiration are called 'those with spirits'. The call usually begins to manifest at an early age, most frequently during the critical period of puberty. The Chukchee say that a potential shaman can be recognized by the look in the eyes which are not directed towards a listener during conversation but seem fixed on something beyond. The eyes also have a strange quality of light, a peculiar brightness which allows them to see spirits and those things hidden from an ordinary person.

The Chukchee use the term 'bashful' to describe the psychological state of both shamans and spirits. By this, according to Bogoras, they mean to convey the highly sensitive psychic state of shamans and the shyness of spirits. 'A shaman of great power will refuse to show his skill when among strangers. He is shy of strange people, a house to which he is not accustomed, of "alien" drums and charms which are hidden in their bags, and of "spirits" that hover around. The least doubt or sneer makes him break off his performance and retire.'[6]

The Chukchee shaman declares that the kelet or spirits belong to the wilderness just as much as any wild animal. This is the reason why they are so 'fleeting'. Kelet of the animal type are the most shy. In one Chukchee tale, the Rheum kelet, gathering up sufficient courage to enter a human dwelling, makes numerous attempts before it successfully overcomes its bashfulness. When caught by a shaman, it fearfully pleads for its freedom.

The sensitivity of spirit and seer is found in other shamanic cultures. For example, the Huichols of Mexico say that the shaman in his peyote trance is very 'delicate'. When the psyche is open and vulnerable, the soul can be stolen or wander away, thus making the individual 'soft to die', a Chukchee expression.

The Chukchee believe that the call to shamanism, if refused or thwarted, can lead to death. In spite of that, there is often a tremendous resistance to pursuing a shamanic vocation. The Chukchee speak of those 'doomed to inspiration', knowing how dangerous is the lifeway of the shaman.

Although the journey is perilous, the ability of the shaman to be in a special and particular relationship with the elements, the creatures of nature, and the spirits from the unseen world, makes the shaman an invaluable member of his or her social network. Through the wisdom and work of the shaman, social and environmental crises can be mitigated and the possibility of survival increased.

Even in more mundane matters the ability of the shaman to control himself, to be disciplined, to know, makes life more bearable. Once, as Cherokee medicine-man Rolling Thunder was collecting herbs, mosquitoes were swarming around him but never touched him. His comment was 'Mosquitoes won't bother you – might not even touch you – if you know how to maintain your good feelings. These attitudes make vibrations; and they have a smell to 'em. That's what keeps the mosquitoes away. You can make a smell they don't care for ... you can control the whole situation by the smell you make – by the vibrations you make. It's not so easy, that kind of control. But it's not impossible because you do it yourself. It's all done from the inside.'[7]

The simple feat of controlling mosquitoes by emitting a particular smell is but one of a myriad of examples of the unusual capacity of shamans to control or trick. Many observers of shamanic seances over the years have doubted the ability of shamans to manipulate weather, perform surgery, suck out sickness, materialize objects, move things at a distance, see into the future, and know the unknowable. Waldemar Bogoras, in the course of his Siberian travels, began to develop a rather cynical attitude toward shaman-magicians. However, an encounter he had with an old shaman from St Lawrence Island convinced him that something out of the ordinary was going on in the case of this eighty-year-old wizard.

In 1901, when I was working among the natives on Bering Sea, I went with a group of Asiatic Eskimos across the channel to St. Lawrence Island, which belongs to the United States. In the village of Chibukak I stayed in the underground house of one Abra, an old man about eighty, quite decrepit and white-haired. White hair among these natives comes only at a very advanced age. Abra was of old Shamanistic stock. In fact, the name of his great grandfather, likewise Abra, was famous in the stories of his tribe, some of which I succeeded in writing down. I asked Abra to show me his Shamanistic skill, but he did not want to comply out of fear of the American Baptist preacher, who was at the same time the chief (and only) official, the physician and the schoolmaster of the village. I got permission from that clerical and civil authority to have a Shamanistic seance, though I had to promise that none of the natives would take part in the fiendish sport. As for the old shaman and myself, the American argued that our reprobate souls could not possibly incur any additional danger.

So we two were left, the shaman and I, in the sleeping-room of his underground house. Abra had removed nearly all of his clothing. He took my best American double blanket and placed two corners of it on his own naked shoulders. The other corners he gave me to hold. 'Do not let

7 Boyd, Rolling Thunder, 133.

them go!' he warned as he began to crawl out of the sleeping-room, which was some ten feet wide. The blanket seemed by some strange power to stick fast to his shoulders. It tightened and I felt the corners that I held on the point of escaping from my hands. I set my feet against a kind of cross-beam that ran along the flooring, but the tension of the blanket almost raised me to my feet, entirely against my will. Then all at once I made a sudden movement and dug both my arms, blanket and all, deep behind the wooden frame that supported the skin cover of the sleeping-room; I and the sleeping-room were practically one. 'Now we shall see,' said I to myself.

The tension continued to increase, and lo, the framed wall rose on both sides of me, right and left. The rays of moonshine entered the room and cut athwart the darkness. A flat tank to the right of me, full of water and half dissolved snow, was overturning and the ice-cold water was spilling on my knees. A heap of iron pans and dishes and ladles and spoons, on my right, was breaking down with much noise and clangor. I had a feeling that in a moment the whole house would tumble in about my ears, and from a sheer instinct of self-preservation I let go of the blanket. It skipped across the space just like a piece of rubber. Then, all at once, I came to myself and looked around. There was no moonshine within the sleeping-room. The water-tank was in its proper place. Likewise pans and dishes. Everything was just as it should be. The awful old shaman had worked on me by will power and made things look queer.

This neat piece of work was the more remarkable in that it was practised on a skeptic like myself who was, so to speak, filled with a spirit of personal resistance against the trickery, and in the absence of the usual crowd of believers, which gives the shaman a terrible tenfold impetus. Abra had been able to curb my will and intelligence altogether singlehanded. And now he was calling from the outer room with a note of exultation. 'But the blanket is for me!' For the objects handled by the spirits become wholly unfit and even dangerous for the use of average human beings, and must be given over to the shaman.[8]

The sacred way of the wounded healer

The opening of vision for the shaman unfolds in a transpersonal realization resulting from a crisis of death and rebirth, a transformation of the profane individual into one who is sacred. For many neophytes, this realization awakens in the dream-web when animal-tutors and spirits of the Other World appear. They come as emissaries of mythical beings, of gods and ancestors. And the candidate is doomed if he or she does not accept the instructions received in the dream from these presences of the Other World.

It is through dreams and visions that the purely sacred is often attained. The rules, regulations, and taboos of the inner life and of a higher natural order are made known. The map of the hidden cosmos is revealed. The paths to and from the realm of death are repeatedly traversed. Animal-

8 *Asia*, New York, XXIX, No. 4 (April 1929), 335–6.

A rock painting on granite depicts the Thunderbird above and a bear shaman with his assistant below. In many Native American cultures, bear medicine was considered to be particularly powerful. For early peoples across the planet the bear was ancestor and god, totem and guardian, medicine-giver and lover. (Drawing, after Campbell Grant, Rock Art of the American Indian, of rock painting from Medicine Rapids, Saskatchewan.)

instructors chant the secrets of the Divine Ones. The Spirit of Night, everywhere present yet nowhere visible, is manifested. The dreamer's soul travels from one sacred mountain to another – the pilgrim being led by a guardian spirit. The owl, coyote, fox, bear, serpent, seal, frog, and lizard enchant in the dream-web. The spirits of dead relatives appear and announce the vocation of the dreamer. Green dwarfs, mushroom-men, clowns and spirit-doctors slip through the dream door to call the dreamer forward on the journey.

The Kwakiutl of the American Northwest Coast say, 'The dreamer is a creature of the shamans, for he listens all the time to learn what the sick people say when they point out the places where they have pains. All this is found out by the dreamers, and they tell this to the shamans of their numayma (village group). For this reason, I call the dreamer the eyes of the shamans.'[1]

The impulse to see and describe the structure of the cosmos everywhere exists for those peoples whose psyches have been opened to the experience of non-ordinary realities. For many shamanic cultures, the universe is believed to be composed of three levels. The Middle Realm is the world as we know it, the world of normal human events. The world below, the Underworld, is associated with the dead and dangerous spirits. And the Overworld, the Celestial Realm, is the abode of the Sun, the realm of transcendent consciousness.

The Underworld has been variously described by shaman-voyagers as a dangerous and terrifying place. The realm of the dead in the many Arctic traditions resembles the world of the living except that all that exists there is upside down or inside out. Death is a reversal of life. According to the tradition of the Siberian Samoyeds, the trees grow downwards, the sun sets in the east and rises in the west, and the rivers flow against their courses. The world, life's phases, and daily human activity are all inverted, like reflections on the surface of a still pond.

The Finns describe the house of the dead as being carpeted with women's hair and supported by men's bones. To get to Tuonela, the Land of the Dead, a black river must be traversed. Neither sun nor moon shines on the River of Death. This gloomy river seems to run north through the Underworld of many cultures. Its dark, boiling waters frequently appear filled with unfortunate souls that writhe as toads and lizards in agony. The bridge connecting the Middle Realm to the Underworld is also ever-present. Some shamanic visions call for the use of a corpse-boat or spirit canoe in traversing these abyssal waters.

Uno Holmberg describes the death-river of the Finns. In Pohjola there flows a dreary river towards the North. This 'awful stream swallows up all water'. There the trees and reeds sink downwards. The rapids in the river are said to be a flaming whirlpool. The gateway to Pohjola is described in magic songs as a place that breeds sickness and death and is guarded by the evil Underworld Mistress who rules a village of maneaters. The inhabitants of Pohjola are those who were killed without sickness, and their garments drip with blood.[2]

On the journey to the Land of Death, the shaman and soul must brave icy winds, burning forests, stormy rivers, and bloody streams. According to the tradition of the Siberian Golds, the soul of the deceased rides a shaman-

1 Boas, *Kwakiutl Ethnography*, 125.

2 Holmberg, *Mythology of All Races*, IV, 51–81.

A Lapp shaman (noidde) in trance
falls beneath his drum as his spirit
journeys to the Other World. In
some accounts the shaman's soul
flies as a whirlwind or fire to the
Other World. The noidde uses the
drum as a means of excitation and
also as an instrument of divination.
(From J. Schefferus, Lapponia,
1673.)

reindeer through this dangerous passage. The areas traversed during the voyage are described by the shaman in songs and ceremonies. The shaman first conducts the soul to the source of a particular river. The two cross to a high mountain range, a primeval forest, and a second great mountain. Beyond this a dangerous swamp has to be navigated. Further the road leads to a mountain torrent where, on the open banks, a beautiful forest grows. Then signs of human life are encountered with felled trees and marks of newly-timbered boats. On the far side of this wood lies the village of the dead.[3]

The Siberian Yakuts face an even greater challenge on their Underworld voyage. The soul or shaman must travel through the throat and body of a serpent-monster. The gullet and bowels of this fantastic creature are lined with great, sharp spikes that would mortally lacerate the traveller if he or she were not provided with shoes and clothing.

The Siberian Altaic shaman enters the gloomiest of forests and traverses the highest of mountains. Everywhere are the bones of shamans and their mounts who have died while voyaging in these forsaken wastelands. At last, the shaman comes upon a hole in the earth and begins the journey in the Underworld Realm. In the Land of the Dead, spirits of disease haunt the shaman, and the souls of transgressors reveal their terrifying fate with violent gestures. The shaman then confronts the Lord of the Underworld, who howls and bellows like a maddened bull. Through trickery and gifts, the shaman appeases this awesome presence. Finally, the shaman returns from the Underworld on the wings of the wild gander – in considerably more style than when he or she embarked on the journey. After undergoing all these trials the shaman is at last able to rescue the souls of others.

The Altaic shaman describes his or her adventures through the ecstatic and theatric action of trance. He or she physically performs the journey while undertaking it on the spiritual plane. The interior state is revealed, made known, and then ultimately exorcized through performance. The venerated images of the awakened psyche are communicated as living symbols in the process of inner spiritual transformations.

The shaman as artist and performer utilizes the imagination to give form to a cosmos that is unpredictable. Even in the course of wild initiatory trances, the mythological rendering of a chaotic psyche is essential. Order is imposed on chaos; form is given to psychic confusion; the journey finds its direction. The shaman also provides a diseased person 'with a language, by means of which unexpressed and otherwise inexpressible psychic states can be immediately expressed. And it is the transition to this verbal expression – at the same time making it possible to undergo in an ordered and intelligible form a real experience that would otherwise be chaotic and

3 Holmberg, Mythology of All Races,
IV, 484–5.

inexpressible – which induces the release of the physiological process.'[4]

Accounts of the shaman's inner journey of turmoil and distress, sung and poeticized, condense personal symbolism through a mythological lens that encompasses the wider human experience. Through creative expression, the human condition is elevated, mythologized, and, at last, collectively understood. Thus a transpersonal language emerges recounting the most intimate and intense of psychic details. Both Claude Lévi-Strauss and Clifford Geertz stress the integrative aspect of the language of myths. The psyche that is emotionally saturated organizes itself by means of mythological conceptions that form an explanatory system which gives significance and direction to human suffering. The seemingly irrational is found to be ordered though paradoxical. The socially unacceptable becomes the stuff of sacred social drama. The extraordinary dangers that are encountered in the psychophysiological adventures of the shaman become at first bearable, and then ultimately heroic.

The shaman, however, is *not* afraid of the universe but feasts on its forces while allowing its forces to feast on him. Sila whispers to the Eskimo neophyte to fear not, yet the dreams and visions of shamans are in general horrifying and elemental. Through the experience of destruction comes instruction. Dismemberment by ravenous spirits allows for the reconstitution of the candidate to a new and higher order of being.

In the Siberian account that follows, the shaman is born of a she-eagle, the Sun Bird, who is an emissary of the Sun. The iron of the eagle's feathers is associated with the origin of fire; it is the striking of iron on stone that brings forth fire. Metallurgical magic implies mastery over fire which the Siberian shaman will attain at the end of the initiation process. The candidate is born in a larch tree and raised by a one-eyed, one-handed, and one-legged spirit-shamaness who then feeds the neophyte to hungry spirits. The act of sacrifice and self-sacrifice prepares the shaman for the life of one who is specially chosen.

> In the far, far north, say the Yakuts, a great larch with many branches stands at the source of terrible sickness. On these branches are nests in which shamans are born. The most powerful shamans receive their training in the nests on the highest of branches. Middling shamans are raised on the middle branches, and little shamans can be found on the lowest branches.
>
> When the shaman is to be born, a great eagle with feathers of iron and hook-like claws flies to the sacred larch and lays an egg. If the shaman is of the highest order, the bird stays with the egg for three long years. If the shaman is of a lower order, the time for nesting and hatching is only one year.
>
> The she-eagle is called 'Mother of Animals'. On three occasions during the lifetime of a shaman does she appear. The first, when she gives birth to the shaman; the second, when the shaman undergoes dismemberment and sacrifice; and the third, when the shaman meets death for the final time.
>
> When the shaman-soul hatches from the egg, the Mother of Animals entrusts the baby shaman to a spirit-shamaness, Burgestez-Udagan, who has one eye, one hand, and one leg. This wondrous creature places her

4 Lévi-Strauss, 'The Effectiveness of Symbolism', 193.

charge in a cradle of iron, rocks him, tends him, and brings him up on pieces of coagulated blood.

When the neophyte has attained the proper age, his shaman-mother turns him over to three horrific black and gaunt spirits who hack his flesh to pieces. They place his head on a pole and scatter his flesh in all directions. Three other spirits take the shaman's jawbone and throw it as an oracle in order to divine the origin of all disease and suffering. If an oracle falls in a proper position, this means that the shaman can help a patient with the affliction in question.[5]

The Yakut old people say of the shaman's power to heal: 'He is able only to help with those ailments whose source or evil spirit has been given its proper share of shaman-flesh.'[6] Great shamans suffer dismemberment three times; little shamans only once. Huge numbers of hungry spirits gather and hack the neophyte to tiny pieces which they share among themselves. Sometimes a shaman's flesh is not sufficient for all ailments. In such a case, the shaman is permitted to work only once for each malady that has not been provided for by a piece of his or her flesh.[7]

If the spirits eat leg flesh, for example, the shaman will be able to cure ailments of the legs. If they eat his or her belly, the shaman will have the ability to heal afflictions of the gut. If the spirits consume the shaman's ear, he or she will have the facility for working with disorders of hearing.

During his field work in Eastern Siberia in the earlier part of this century, Lev Shternberg collected numerous accounts of the difficult psycho-physiological manifestations experienced by shaman-candidates. A Gilyak shaman whom Shternberg knew reported that before he became a shaman, he had been ill for nearly three months. During this time, he was unconscious, lying motionless. When the man was nearly dead from exhaustion as a result of his comatose state, he began to dream that he was singing shaman-songs. One evening a white owl appeared close behind him, along with a man who told him, 'Make yourself a drum and all the equipment a shaman needs. Sing shaman-songs. You will never succeed in being an ordinary individual. If you accept the calling of the shaman, you will become one.' The candidate, according to Shternberg, had no idea how long he slept. When he awoke, he found that he was being held over a fire. His relatives believed that the spirits had killed him. He then ordered his relatives to give him a drum, and he began to sing. All fear and doubt had left him.

The shaman, unafraid, experiences death in order to gain control over the elements and the world of the untamed. The withdrawal into solitude through sickness opens the way for the inner initiation to take place. Myth in this case evolves from the ground of the diseased body-mind.

A shaman of the Yaralde tribe of Australia describes the terrors that he encountered during the initiation process:

When you lie down to see the prescribed visions, and you do not see them, do not be frightened, because they will be horrible. They are hard to describe, though they are in my mind and my *miwi* (i.e., psychic force), and though I could project the experience into you after you had been well trained.

Among the Dayak of Borneo, it is believed that the spirit of a dead person can fly to unearthly realms in the form of a bee. The idea of the soul taking the form of an insect is found in various parts of the world, including Mexico. (Drawing after Eliot, Myths.*)*

5 See Lommel, *Shamanism: The Beginnings of Art,* 55.

6 See ibid., 57.

7 See ibid., 55.

However, some of them are evil spirits, some are like snakes, some are like horses with men's heads, and some are spirits of evil men which resemble burning fires. You see your camp burning and the blood waters rising, and thunder, lightning and rain, the earth rocking, the hills moving, the waters whirling, and the trees which still stand, swaying about. Do not be frightened. If you get up, you will not see these scenes, but when you lie down again, you will see them, unless you get too frightened. If you do, you will break the web (or thread) on which the scenes are hung. You may see dead persons walking towards you, and you will hear their bones rattle. If you hear and see these things without fear, you will never be frightened of anything. These dead people will not show themselves to you again, because your *miwi* is now strong. You are now powerful because you have seen these dead people.[8]

The retreat to Paradise

For some shamans, the means of ascent from the abyss of the Underworld is the Cosmic Tree, a symbol of perpetual regeneration. This great tree stands at the very centre of the universe directing the vision of a culture skyward towards the eternally sacred.

All life springs from the primeval waters that flow from the tree and gather at its base, waters which are limitless, an essential sea circulating through all of nature. These waters are the beginning and end of all existence, the ever-moving matrix that nurtures and preserves life. The World Tree, expressing its milky golden sap, denotes 'absolute reality', a return to the centre and place of origin, the home of wisdom that heals.

In the folk tradition of the Siberian Yakuts, as related by Uno Holmberg, a dense tree with eight branches stands on the yellow navel of the eight-edged earth. The bark and knots of this tree are of silver, its sap is golden, and from its branches hang cones like nine-cornered goblets. The leaves of this wondrous tree are as broad as the hide of a horse. From its crown there runs a foaming golden sap that quenches the thirst and abates the hunger of those that drink of this heavenly nectar.

It is this tree with its life-giving waters that binds all realms together. The roots of the World Tree penetrate the depths of the Underworld. The body of the tree transects the Middle World. And the crown embraces the heavens.

'In a number of archaic traditions,' states Eliade, 'the Cosmic Tree . . . is related to the idea of creation, fecundity, and initiation, and finally to the idea of absolute reality and immortality. . . . The World Tree is a tree that *lives and gives life*.'[1] This Cosmic Tree, like the Bo Tree under which the Buddha attained enlightenment, or the sublime tree of the Hindus that shaded Yama, the first man, as he drank with the gods, harbours the inexhaustible spring of human life, the means of attaining immortality. It is an *arbor vitae*, a Tree of Life, as well as a Tree of Knowledge. Through the body of the tree, life and death are joined, as are the heavens and the Underworld. The unifying significance of the Cosmic Tree can also be seen in the shaman's ladder which is used for ascents to the celestial realms.

8 Eliade, *Shamanism*, 86.

1 Eliade, *Shamanism*, 271–2.

Among the Mapuche of Chile, the *rewe* (or carved pole) and the drum are the shaman's two most prominent pieces of equipment. The drum is beaten by the shaman for long periods of time and induces a deep trance. It is the means of attaining non-ordinary consciousness, as the *rewe* is the means of attaining the realm of spirits. The faces and breasts carved on the notched pole are said to represent spirit familiars which are ancestral shamans (see p. 85).

The initiation of the Mapuche shaman (usually a woman) centres on ritual climbing of the *rewe*. A nine-foot tree is stripped of its bark and notched to form a ladder. It is then placed in the ground in front of the house of the neophyte shaman. The candidate undresses to her undergarments and lies down on a couch where an old *machi* or shaman rubs her with canelo and makes passes over her body. A chorus of shamans chant and ring bells during the course of this procedure. According to Alfred Métraux, the elder women bend over the initiate and suck her breasts, belly, and head with such force that blood is drawn.

The following day, many guests arrive as the ceremony is nearing its climax. The candidate and her attendants approach the *rewe* where the young woman, followed by her elders, ascends the seven levels of the tree as they dance and drum.

According to another account, prior to the ascent, lambs are sacrificed and the heart of one of the sacrificed beasts is hung from a branch of a brush enclosure. In a deep trance state, a blindfolded shaman uses a white quartz knife to draw blood from the candidate as well as from herself, which she mixes together. Then the troop of shamans make their ascent up the *rewe* accompanied by continuous chanting and drumming. The apprentice is stripped of a necklace of greenery and a bloodstained lamb's fleece before the descent from the *rewe* takes place. When the group has accomplished the descent, the newly initiated shaman is greeted with a tremendous uproar. A feast completes the ritual.

The climbing of trees in the process of shamanic initiation can be found in Malaysia, Siberia, the Americas, and Australia, where an interesting variation of this practice is described by R. Berndt and A. P. Elkin: 'A Wongaibon lying on his back at the foot of a tree, sent his cord directly up and "climbed" up with his head well back, body outstretched, legs apart, and arms to his sides. Arriving at the top, forty feet up, he waved his arms to those below, and then came down in the same manner, and while still on his back the cord re-entered his body.'[2]

The bridge connecting the earth and sky, for the Australian medicine-man as well as for shamans in other cultures, can be the rainbow. Eliade points out that the coloured ribbons used in Siberian Buryat initiations are called 'rainbows'; they represent the shaman's voyage to the Sky Realm. Shaman drums from various cultures are painted with drawings of the rainbow as a bridge to the Other World. In the Turkic language the word for rainbow and bridge is the same. The shaman drum among the Yurak-Samoyed of Siberia is called 'bow'. By the same token, the magic of the shaman as well as the drum is able to project him or her to the Sky Realm like an arrow. Thus, the Cosmic Tree, the drum, the hunting-bow and rainbow all become roads to the Heaven Realm. So also do chains of arrows, vines, cords, stairs and ladders, bridges and holy mountains.

2 Elkin, *Aboriginal Men of High Degree*, 64.

To fly as birds

In the beginning, according to a tale of the Siberian Buryats, there existed gods in the West and evil spirits in the East. The gods created human beings who knew nothing about sickness and death. Nevertheless, misfortune or illness could descend on people through the work of evil spirits. The gods in the sky saw this suffering and sent an eagle to earth to assist and protect. Thus the eagle was the first shaman. The people, however, did not understand the mission of the Sun Bird. They could not interpret its speech or its ways; and so the eagle was forced to return to the celestial realm. Upon its return to the place of the gods, the eagle was instructed to journey back to the earth and give its shaman nature to the first person that it encountered. And so the eagle made its return voyage to the Middle World. As it approached a wooded area, the bird saw a woman sleeping beneath a tree. She had left her husband and was quite alone. The eagle transmitted his essence to the woman, who became pregnant. The woman returned to her husband and gave birth to a son, the first human shaman.[1]

For the Buryats of Siberia, the eagle is the prototype of the shaman. The Gilyaks of Siberia have the same word for eagle and shaman. The Yenissei Ostyaks believe that the first shaman was a two-headed eagle. The Teleuts say that the eagle is a shaman-bird, because it assists the shaman in his or her celestial ascent. Some Siberian peoples directly associate the eagle with the Supreme Being and the Creator of Light. Similarly, among the Finns, the first shaman, Vainamoinen, was descended from an eagle. Odin was also called eagle.

The eagle and the shaman are both intercessors between gods and human beings. In essence, the shaman, born of an eagle father who is an emissary of the Creator of Light, becomes an eagle and returns to the place of origin. In ascents to the celestial regions, the shaman attempts to turn into a bird and fly. Among the Eskimo, the shaman flies to the Upper and Lower Worlds as a representative of those on earth. The shaman may attempt such flights for the good of the community or out of pure pleasure. The Eskimo shaman Samik relates a story of his grandfather's playful spirit flights:

> My grandfather was from Netsilik Land; he was very fond of going out on spirit flights, and once when he was out there he met another great shaman from Utkuhikjalik, a man named Muraoq, who was·also out on a spirit flight. They met far out over the sea ice, about midway between their villages. When the two met, Muraoq spread out his arms like a bird gliding on its wings, but he was incautious and came so close to Titqatsaq that they collided in the air; they crashed together so violently that Titqatsaq fell down on the ice. He lay there without being able to move until Muraoq turned back and got his helping spirit to help him up again. Scarcely had Titqatsaq got up into the air again when he returned the compliment and crashed against Muraoq, so that he, too, dropped on the ice. At first he thought of leaving him without helping him up; but then he recalled how often Muraoq had been good to him; that was why

1 See Lommel, *Shamanism: The Beginnings of Art*, 111.

Although it might appear that shamans are only involved in serious endeavours, there are numerous instances of clowning, joking, and wild play by shamans. Here two Eskimo wizards fly for sport as well as spirit. One of them, unable to keep up, falls to the earth and begs his competitor to stop. (From Rasmussen, Eskimo Folk Tales.*)*

he took pity on him, flew back and helped him up in exactly the same way as he himself had been helped up; and when they got home they told the people at their villages all that had happened.[2]

Whether for sport or spirit, the shaman's ability to fly or the enactment of flight bespeaks a sublime metaphysical reality that appears to be a common feature of mystical experiences everywhere.

Not only does the shaman fly, so also do various animal allies – bear, deer, horse, and feathered serpent – who carry the shaman to the Above and the Below. Bird song can also be the vehicle of flight, transporting the mage to wonders far beyond the imaginings of those who are earthbound. Goose and gander, swan, hawk and eagle, parrot, anhinga, dove, and condor – birds that ravage and eat the meat of sacrifice, predator-birds, birds of keen sight and power, birds of song and serenity – winged angels and demons flying through mythologies of cultures everywhere: their seed form is found in the psyche of the shaman.

To the heavens, to the well at the end of the world, to the depths of the Underworld, to the bottoms of spirit-filled lakes and seas, around the earth, to the moon and sun, to distant stars and back again does the shaman-bird travel. All the cosmos is accessible when the art of transformation has been mastered.

The Sun Door

The journey's mythic end is the sun. The shaman flies through the Sun Door to the realm of eternally awakened consciousness. The very act of sacrifice in the domesticated fire of initiation makes it possible for the sacrificed one to enter the realm of the immortal. The solar region is beyond time and space. Those who have died and been reborn have realized the dual unity of the mortal and immortal aspects of human existence. The fire of transformation has burned away all that is transient. The raw Sun then receives the immortal's liberated spirit.

In many mythologies, the father above is the sun. In some Siberian tales, the first shaman is the eagle or Sun Bird. The shaman's transformation via fire into a master of fire allows for a parallel transformation of neophyte shaman into soaring bird – Sun Bird – and a return to the source – the sun or Sun Father. Mortal and immortal, human and animal, piercing the dual unity, the

2 Rasmussen, *The Netsilik Eskimos,* 299–300.

shaman becomes not only a solar traveller but also a vehicle of fire.

The North American Lakota, greeting the sun upon its rising, call out:

> *here am I*
> *behold me*
> *I am the sun*
> *behold me*[1]

The Sun Door that has received the sacrificed shaman is the very gate that opens within when the psyche is deeply awakened. The illumined ones are often depicted with haloes or aureoles shimmering around their heads and bodies. The Sun has been introjected, internalized. The inner light has been revealed through the action of a self-achieved submission. The external sun in effect has consumed the body of the sacrificed one, whose bones are held in the embrace of the sun-vessel. Sacrifice to the sun, whether in the physical expression that releases the spirit during the Lakota Sun Dance, or in prayer offerings by the Huichols to the Sun, Tayaupa, is a celebration that honours all of life. In the act of sacrifice, sacredness is accomplished, for nothing returns to its former state once given up.

> *No mirror becomes iron again*
> *No ripe grape becomes sour again*[2]

This is a drawing from a Siberian shaman's drum. The central figure, with power lines or rays emanating from around its head, could be a celestial spirit or a shaman who has gone through the process of solarization. (From Istorio Etnograficheskii Atlas Sibirii, *Moscow, 1961.)*

The shaman is self-slain through the surrender of all that is transient, becoming like a great field that is plowed, ripped open for seed to be planted.

Raw sun and domesticated fire are one in essence. Slayer and slain are one. As such the mastery of fire is the shaman's play with the Absolute. Shamans and wizards the world over relate directly to fire as a demonstration of this mastery and a manifestation of their faith.

Fire is thus directly experienced with the aid of the images contained within the psyche. The rational mind rejects the possibility of actually engaging fire. And yet, shaman and ecstatic transcend the limitations of nature and historical precedent to enact the psychological image in the flesh. A mutation of the real takes place through a living symbolic process of the inner becoming the outer.

The relationship between friction, combustion, fire, heat, and light is the analogue of the initiation process and its outcome. The Vedic term *śram* means 'to heat oneself'. The shaman is one who has been heated through the friction of initiation, and in the burning process has become the pure light. Crystals and rainbows also come into the picture here. The shaman's crystal is the boneseed of rebirth, a repository as well as transceiver of illumination. For the Huichols, the crystal, as power object, has encoded within it the soul of a deceased shaman who becomes instructor to the living shaman, one who gives power and light. The rainbow performs much the same function in the sense that it is a bridge to the Other World. Through self-sacrifice, the shaman is able to cross the Rainbow Bridge to the Realm of the Gods.

The shaman, supreme master of fire, is the embodiment of a heat so fierce that its spiritual luminescence is associated with both purity and

1 *Parabola*, Tamarack Press, New York, III, No. 2 (1978), 44.

2 Ibid.

knowledge. An Eskimo shaman explained this to Knud Rasmussen in the following way: 'Every real shaman has to feel an illumination in his body, in the inside of his head or in his brain, something that gleams like fire, that gives him the power to see with closed eyes into the darkness, into the hidden things or into the future, or into the secrets of another man. I felt that I was in possession of this marvelous ability.'[3]

The longing for illumination on the part of those overwhelmed by darkness opens the way, and the journey begins. The shaman and seer drink from the dangerous cup of immortality to know death as life and life as death. What was vulnerable, wounded, is now immortalized.

> We have drunk the soma and become immortal!
> We have attained the light, we have found the Gods.
> What can the malice of mortal man
> or his spirit, O immortal, do to us now?
>
> Make me shine brightly like fire produced by friction.
> Illumine us, make us ever more prosperous
> Enthused by you, Soma, I find myself rich!
> Enter within us for our well-being.[4]

The return to the people

The mythic journey climaxes in the solar realm. The life journey for a Holy One culminates in the return from Paradise to society. The shaman's vocation focuses on the people – and too long a stay in the realm of the Gods can make the return impossible. Through the encounter with death and the knowledge of the pairs of opposites, the shaman has attained the wisdom of the 'two-worlds'. Lakota medicine-man, Leonard Crow Dog, speaks of a reality behind the apparent reality. Knowing this, then, the unity underlying the separate and divided forms is revealed. Huichol shaman Ramon Medina Silva once said, 'It is one, it is a unity, it is ourselves.' The shaman, through sacred action, reveals this unity. It is the way of compassion that opens in the course of this revelation.

The shaman then is a master of play, dancing, and chanting in the field of human suffering. And through these acts, the people are awakened from the nightmare of sickness to the dream of Paradise. Playfulness and absurdity sharply rouse the slumbering ones. The beauty of poetry and the ferocity of keen wisdom remind the forgetful ones. Compassion and poise heal the diseased ones. The world is revealed, remembered, and celebrated. The ancestors and Nature-Kin are again in the sacred circle.

'While I stood there, I saw more than I can tell, and I understood more than I saw; for I was seeing in a sacred manner the shapes of all things in the spirit, and the shape of all shapes as they must live together like one being.'[1]

The essence of life

The Huichol shaman, Ramon Medina Silva, explained to anthropologist Peter Furst that the life energy force or *kupuri* of a deceased elder was the

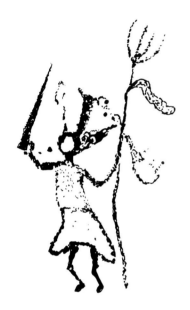

A carved figure, carrying a planting stick and corn, seems to bound and dance in timeless space. The wizard dancer of the fields brings abundance to the harvest, for it is through celebration and praise that the plants flourish. (Drawing, after Wellmann, 1979, of a rock carving, Rio Grande style, West Mesa, Albuquerque, New Mexico.)

3 Quoted in Lommel, *Shamanism: The Beginnings of Art*, 60.

4 *Parabola*, Tamarack Press, New York, III, No. 2 (1978), 44.

1 Neihardt, *Black Elk Speaks*, 43.

only soul capable of returning to the world of the living. The Huichols believe that five years after one has died, the soul of the deceased can rejoin the living in the form of a rock crystal. In this crystallized state, the soul is called *tewari*, meaning grandfather or ancestor. Ramon insisted that not all souls are capable of manifesting as rock crystals.

> Only the souls who were sixty, seventy years old, the old people, those with wisdom, come back. Not those who died at twenty-five or at thirty, those not. Because they are not yet complete, they are not wise, they are not *mara'akate* (shamans) or other wise people. They do not have the complete years; they died incomplete. Those more than fifty, those, yes. They have experience, wisdom, knowledge. Those come back after five years. Men that are sturdy, that have learned well, that have taken heed, with much energy and strength, their thoughts filled with much wisdom. And the same for women, women who are wise, who have gone for the peyote, who have knowledge, all these, yes.[1]

The life of the ancestor can thus be reconstituted in the form of a rock crystal which has been created from five particles of bone of the skeletal remains of the deceased. In this way, the old one returns to the living as a guardian spirit and guarantor of the hunt.

In Australia, the rock crystals introduced into neophytes' bodies in the course of shamanic initiation, like the Huichol *tewari*, originate in the environs of the sun. According to the Huichols, 'It is into this dangerous sphere, flooded with blinding light and scorching heat, that the *mara'akame* ventures in order to procure the ancestral soul with the aid of the tutelary spirit helper, the Sacred Deer *Kauyumari*.'[2] The ancestral soul of the Huichol elder-shaman is captured by a living *mara'akame* in the fermented maize drink called *nawa*. 'And the owner of the deer snare comes close and drinks the *nawa*, the *nawa* in which the crystal was. In which it was caught. It is he who drinks all this *nawa*.'[3] In effect, the shaman who drinks the *nawa* in which is found the *tewari*, is drinking liquor containing the symbolic bones of a deceased elder-shaman.

There is much evidence of endo-cannibalism in the Americas and Australia where bones and clothing of the deceased are made into drinks and imbibed. In this way, the bond between the living and the dead is revitalized. The crystal, then, as a reincarnated elder, is not only a protector of the hunt, but also a teacher of the living shaman. The *tewari* advises the *mara'akame* on the proper manner in which to conduct ceremonies, the hunt, and life in the village. In effect, the shaman is apprenticed to the *tewari*.[4]

Another point Furst makes is that the 'owner of the deer snare', the one who has drunk the bone liquor of the *tewari*, is an elder and headman of a village. In former times, headmen were usually *mara'akame* as well. These roles are identified with *Tatewari*, Our Grandfather Fire, who is not only the tutelary deity of shamans but also the first shaman. This leads us to the notion that the continuity between the living, the wise dead, and ancestral nature spirits is a primary course for the shaman, who is not only intercessor between spirit and human but also a medium for forces from the Other World. The shaman is thus the channel for the knowledge of the Ancients,

1 Furst, 'Huichol Conceptions of the Soul', 80.

2 Ibid., 93.

3 Ibid., 93.

4 Ibid., 93.

the means by which the wisdom of the elders and elements is transmitted to the community.[5]

For the Huichols, the first ancestor was *Tatewari*. In the Paradisical Era before the flood, when people, creatures, divine beings, and gods were not differentiated from each other, he was brought into being by the *Hewixi*, animal-people who later were drowned in the great flood that destroyed the world. *Apii*, the ancestral shaman-chief of the *Hewixi*, rubbed two sticks together and from them was brought forth fire, *Tatewari*, which was contained within the wood. Because fire 'came forth' first in the world, he is called Our Grandfather.

There is much affection for Our Grandfather Fire among the Huichols. Anthropologist Barbara Myerhoff notes that on a practical level, *Tatewari*, as fire, clears the fields, cooks the foods, and provides warmth and light. He transmutes the raw and makes a civilized life possible. He also symbolically stands for companionship; where he is, so also are Huichols. As the oldest god among the Huichols, the first *mara'akame*, and the shaman of the Ancient Ones, *Tatewari* protects and transmits the traditions of long ago. He is much loved by the Huichols for he reveals the unknowable with his light and his wisdom of great age.

The text that follows was given to Dr Myerhoff by the Huichol shaman, Ramon Medina Silva. The narrative reveals the profound significance of this first elder of Ancient Times:

Why do we adore the one who is not of this world, whom we call *Tatewari*, the one who is the Fire? We have him because we believe in him in this form. *Tai*, that is fire, only fire, flames. *Tatewari* that is the Fire. That is the *mara'akame* from ancient times, the one who warms us, who burns the brush, who cooks our food, who hunted the deer, the peyote, that one who is with Kauyumari. We believe in him. Without him, where would we get warmth? How would we cook? All would be cold. To keep warm Our Sun Father would have to come close to the earth. And that cannot be so.

Imagine. One is in the Sierra, there where we Huichols live. One walks, one follows one's paths. Then it becomes dark. One is alone there walking; one sees nothing. What is it there in the dark? One hears something? It is not to be seen. All is cold. Then one makes camp there. One gathers a little wood, food for Tatewari. One strikes a light. One brings out Tatewari. Ah, what a fine thing! What warmth! What light! The darkness disappears. It is safe. Tatewari is there to protect one. Far away, another walks. He sees it. There he is, walking all alone in the darkness, afraid perhaps. Then he sees it from far away, that light, that friendly light. A friendly thing in the dark. He says, 'I am not alone. There is another Huichol. There is someone. Perhaps he has a place for me there, a little warmth.' So he speaks. Tatewari is there in the dark, making light, making one warm, guarding one. Is it possible to live without such a thing, without Tatewari? No, it is not possible.

Or if it is a matter of working to produce maize, squash, beans, melon. Working is not enough. We need Tatewari. If one has a wife, she wishes to cook for one. How can one satisfy one's hunger with a pot of raw beans? With raw maize? It does not satisfy. But give these things into the hands

5 Ibid., 93.

of Tatewari, let them be warmed by the flower of his flames, then it is well. In Ancient Times he was transformed. When the Ancient Ones brought him out, he came out as *mara'akame*, transformed, so that all could see him as he was. So that he could embrace Our Father when he was born. So that he could lead those Ancient Ones who were not of this world to hunt the deer, to hunt peyote. So that Kauyumari and he became companions, so that our life, our customs could be established there from Ancient Times, so long ago that no one can remember when it was.

That is why we adore him, why we have him in the center, that one who is Our Grandfather.[6]

A Huichol myth relates that *Tatewari*, one day, found the gods in the *xiriki* or temple complaining bitterly about their ills. They knew not what caused their suffering nor how to rid themselves of disease. Grandfather Fire, desiring to help them, divined that the gods had not made the sacred pilgrimage to *Wirikuta*, the Land of Peyote, for many years. They had forgotten the ways of their ancestors, who had journeyed far to hunt the Deer (peyote) in Paradise, the place of their origin. Forgetting their traditions and obligations to the Divine Ones, so also had they forgotten that to heal they must eat the miraculous flesh of the deer-peyote. And in this way does the *mara'akame*, as Our Grandfather, lead all pilgrims to Paradise to find their Life.

The Huichol shaman's tutelary deity is *Tatewari*; so also is the *mara'akame* identified as Our Grandfather Fire. Like *Tatewari* of the Huichols, Old Woman Momoy of the Southern California Chumash is identified as a mythological ancestor with shaman powers. She is Grandmother Datura, a wealthy widow whose medicine revives the dead and cures the sick. By drinking the water in which she has bathed, one can avoid death. She sets down the rules of conduct and is the guardian of traditions. Her grandson, an orphan whom she raises, grows up to be a powerful shaman and hunter.

Anthropologist Thomas Blackburn notes that age, like knowledge, is highly valued in Chumash society, and, in fact, the two are correlated. With age comes wisdom, and from wisdom comes power. Only the wise can survive to a very old age in a universe that is so dangerous. In the mythology of the Chumash, most characters with power are elderly. Sun, the most powerful of the entities, is depicted as an extremely old man. The elder, Eagle, an influential and rarely visible presence, is characterized as both wise and good, the embodiment of normative values. Well-to-do Eagle, as Chief, has great prestige and provides for the community. The one who administers Datura to pubescent boys is Old Man Coyote, a trickster and a shaman who can change his appearance at will. As Blackburn says, authority and power are a direct function of seniority and maturity.[7]

For many Native American peoples, the status of the aged is one of respect and honour: as one California Pomo has said, 'The old people were important. They were wise.' Living to a ripe old age was a privilege granted by the gods or the Supreme Maker. A life that had been 'completed' was one that had passed through *all* stages to the last, the age of wisdom.

It is the elders who have the greatest access to the ancestors and gods. Many years of practice in the ways of the sacred, combined with the nearing of death, have opened their lives to a manner of spiritual and social freedom.

6 Myerhoff, *Peyote Hunt*, 78–80.

7 Blackburn (ed.), *December's Child*, 74–5.

A radiant spirit being emanating tremendous energy is connected with a headless figure by a power line that goes from the entity's fontanel to the navel area of the human. This could be interpreted as a direct transmission of power from a spirit ally to shaman-recipient. (Drawing, after Wellmann, 1979, of a rock painting, Menomini territory, Manistique, Michigan.)

Those who have been favoured with long life, from one point of view, have gone through a life-span initiation. The path of life itself when traversed with 'an obedience to awareness' is instruction.

The Gros Ventres of Montana believe the elders to be favoured, and from the Wise Ones blessings are sought. 'If you are good to old people, these in turn will pray to the Supreme Being for your health, long life, and success. Children were instructed explicitly to be good to the aged, to feed them, to clothe and to help them in difficulties, as well as to seek out those so blessed and ask for their prayers.'[8]

This change of worlds can be accomplished in life as well as in death. The shaman and the elders understand the fundamental nature of the transformative process. To attain the solar realm where consciousness is eternally awakened, to climb to the top of the mountain where the infinite is revealed, to seek life in order to know death, this is the quest, the journey.

As a child in his Pueblo village, Alfonso Ortiz's vision was directed to the mountaintop, the place where the paths of those living and the dead converge. It is this sacred geography that the shaman attains, and there also are found the ancestors.

A wise elder among my people, the Tewa, frequently used the phrase *Pin pe obi*, 'look to the mountaintop,' while he was alive. I first heard it 25 years ago when I was seven years old; as I was practicing for the first time to participate in relay races we run in the Pueblo country to give strength to the sun father as he journeys across the sky. I was at one end of the earth track which ran east to west, like the path of the sun. The old man who was blind, called to me and said, 'Young One, as you run, look to the mountaintop.' And he pointed to *Taikomo*, the western sacred mountain of the Tewa world, which loomed off in the distance. 'Keep your gaze fixed on that mountain, and you will feel the miles melt beneath your feet. Do this and in time you will feel as if you can leap over bushes, trees, and even the river.' I tried to understand what this last statement meant, but I was too young.

On another occasion a few days later, I asked him if I really could learn to leap over treetops. He smiled and said, 'Whatever life's challenges you may face, remember always look to the mountaintop, for in so doing you look to greatness. Remember this, and let no problem, however great it may seem, discourage you. This is the one thought I want to leave you with. And in that dim coming time when we shall meet again, it shall be on the mountaintop.' Again I wondered why he was telling me these words and what they meant. I did not have long to wonder why, for the following month, when the cornstalks were sturdy on the land, he died quietly in his sleep having seen eighty-seven summers.

Although he knew I was too young to understand, he also knew there was not much time left to impart this message to me and, perhaps, to others like me. In accordance with our beliefs, the ancestors were waiting for him at the edge of the village that day he died, waiting to take him on a final four-day journey to the four sacred mountains of the Tewa world. A Tewa must either be a medicine man in a state of purity or he must be dead before he can safely ascend the sacred mountain. This final journey always ends when the ancestral spirits and the one who has returned

8 Cooper, *The Gros Ventres of Montana: Part II, Religion and Ritual*, 195.

enter a lake near the top of any of the sacred mountains, for these lakes are the homes of the gods.

In the most basic, transcendental sense, then, life for a Tewa consists of trying to fathom the meaning of these words, 'look to the mountaintop,' for they contain a guiding vision of life, a vision evolved through untold millennia of living on this land. Only in recent years have I come fully to realize that this was a priceless gift, for it sums up a people's knowledge of what it means to be of a time and of a place, also beyond time and place. Yet I also know that I shall never fully understand all that is meant by these words, for if ever I or anyone living should do so, it would be time to rejoin the ancestors, to make the last journey to the mountaintop.[9]

All of life for an elder or Holy One is directed toward the attainment of the mountaintop, where a transtemporal geography reveals the infinite. Even the very young are reminded of this sacred possibility. In a Navajo blessing for a child, the medicine-man prays that the little one will grow up healthy and strong into the age of wisdom. The blessing concludes with these words: 'I am the Essence of Life which is old age.'

The end of time

The primordial mythological age, when men and women awakened to create of their dreams and visions coherent, transmittable reckonings, the time when they gave names and shapes to the energies of nature and the cosmos, when the inexplicable and secretly felt gods were given faces and forms, that epoch of millennia has come to an end. The archaic myths were borne across vast geographical territories and enormous spans of time, preserved and transmitted through numberless generations. Superficially, these traditions transformed in response to history and geography; and in time – in our generation – it appears as though we are witnesses to the painful demise of the ancient gods. Nietzsche's Zarathustra proclaimed the death of all the gods, and the obituaries of local deities can be read in our daily newspapers as the impact of Western culture is felt around the planet. Even as the old gods are diminishing, the seers and prophets of the ancient times are yet alive; and for a brief period, a decade, perhaps two, we can embrace the entire sacred history of our planet before it dissolves in the powerful presence of the biomechanical, transindustrial age that is now upon us. Tens of thousands of years of history, yet alive, but predictably to die – and this century is the threshold of its passing. And so we turn our heads to regard our living heritage, perhaps for the last time, to explore the lifeways transmitted to us from the healer-priests of the Palaeolithic, to know their traditions, and to be introduced to the lineage of primordial visionaries that is perhaps coming to an end – or perhaps is to be renewed in a form not yet fully known.

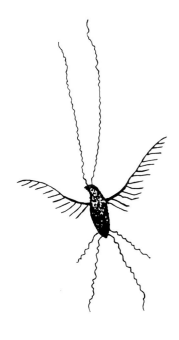

A rock painting in red pigment, of a delicate bird with power lines emanating from its head and tail, portrays the radiant 'life energy force'. (Drawing of rock painting, Garden Peninsula, Fayette State Park, near Manistique, Michigan.)

9 Ortiz, 'Look to the Mountaintops', 95–7.

Descent to the realm of the dead,
home of disease spirits, speaks to
the fundamental helplessness of
humanity. Encountered in the
depths are ravenous spirits that
instruct as they destroy. The
shaman's receptivity to the world of
creatures opens after he or she has
surrendered to death. The face on
this wooden mask has a startled
expression. The eyes are open wide,
yet expressionless, as though the
'wits' have been frightened out of
the subject. Perhaps the neophyte is
dead; or he has suffered a seizure
(epilepsy is often associated with
shamanism). The extruded tongue
also tastes the wisdom of those who
inhabit the wilderness realms.
Claude Lévi-Strauss calls this transmission process the 'kiss of
knowledge': the shaman partakes of
the raw nectar of the world of
creatures. Raw death and a non-
dualistic, amoral universe are
revealed. There is no morality in the
stare of the hawk; nor is there
morality in death. By wearing this
mask, the shaman reminds the
people of this fundamental condition of existence. (Painted wooden
mask of the shaman Seton, Tlingit,
Northwest Coast.)

34

The Eskimo shaman does not exercise his or her special art in private. The objective of the initiation ordeals and of the ritual performances is ultimately that of service to the community. Although shamans go through individual experiences in the solitudes while seeking inspiration, the wilderness is brought back to the people in the form of ceremonies. Among the Eskimo it is believed that people create their own misfortune by breaking taboos. Public confessions, as well as community participation in the shamanic seance, are necessary elements in the release of tensions, as well as in creating the ground for a total cleansing. The beat of the shaman's drum binds together all the elements of the ritual, as well as the separate individuals, into a unified field. The steady repetition of the resonant tones of the drum creates a trance state that has a dynamic impact on all participants. The drawing portrays an entire community in a state of trance-rapture as the shaman

does his work. ('People Stunned by the Drum', by Luke Anguhadluq (b. 1895), drawing, Baker Lake, Eskimo, 1972.)

The Siberian Yakut shaman sings 'The drum is my horse', as its beat carries him or her to the Other World. The drum is also the shaman's territory. Painted on this Teleut drum is a map of the worlds that open to the shaman-traveller. In the lower field is the Old Man of the Threshold, master and protector of the dwelling. Beneath him are offering 'cups' for the gods and spirits. The upper field, the heavenly realm, is bordered by a curved strip enclosing triangles to represent the mountains and powers above. Horses and birds are the shaman's envoys. Near the top of the drum are cages used by shamans to catch spirit-birds, the guardians of heavenly beings. The sun with its morning star and the moon with its evening star adorn the heavenly field, as do the constellations. (Drawing after S.I. Ivanov, 1954.)

The shaman descends to the Underworld to retrieve a patient's soul. He reads the inscription on a magical stone and navigates the river of death in a seven-oared boat, dodging the fish-weirs and rods of the spirits. He is winged, radiant with energy; his antlered head bespeaks his attainment of wisdom. (Drawing, Ostiak-Samoyed, Siberia, from *Asia*, XXIX, No. 4 (1929).)

The Bon-po religion of Tibet is a native tradition associated with shamanism that has syncretized with Indo-Tibetan tantrism. Shamanic motifs, such as dismemberment, being devoured by demons, supernatural ascents and flights, magical heat, spirit possession, soul loss and retrieval, and mystical raptures, are all commonly found in Lamaistic practice. In fact, Lamaism has preserved much of the early Bon tradition. The Ladakh lama-shaman in the photograph, *left*, performs a healing rite. He is dressed in Buddhist garb and uses his bell 'to bring up' the life force of his patient as he himself is in trance. (Photo by Robert G. Gardner, 1978.)

This photograph of Don José (Matsuwa), a Huichol shaman from El Colorín, Municipio del Nayar (Nayarit), high in the Mexican Sierras, was taken during the annual Ceremony of the Drum. The shaman, in trance, opens his heart and mind to the mystery of his sung prayer. Even as he chants, his spirit travels to Wirikuta, the paradise of his people. He flies to this holy desert in the company of the spirits of the village children for whom this ceremony is held. Clutched in Matsuwa's left hand is a prayer arrow which he uses for healing and seeing. He lost his right hand in an accident in his thirties, and it was then that his true initiation took place. (Photo by Prem Das.)

The figure on this Salish (Cowichan) spindle whorl calls to mind the image of the shaman who is reduced to a boneseed after enduring initiatory ordeals. On either side of the central figure are three birds, possibly ravens, and an otter. These figures could well represent the spirit allies of the wearer or of the central figure. Raven is Trickster and Transformer, the culture hero who created the world, and is an ally of the shaman. Like Raven, Otter is also a creature associated with transformation: Otter changes people into creatures. (Carved, painted wooden disc, Salish culture, Northwest Coast, collected 1884.)

This ground-painting (*ilbantera*) of the Northern Aranda of Australia represents the waterhole or 'soak' which is the birthplace of Ilbalintja, the Sun, and of Karora, the bandicoot totem ancestor. It is believed that all life emanated from this place, and it was here that Karora returned after he had completed his earthly wanderings, to sink down to his eternal sleep. The circular head-dresses represent the Sun, and the central actor carries the bandicoot headgear. The ground-painting itself is a sacred gateway to the Other World. It symbolizes the feminine earth, from whose fertile womb the earth-bound deities sprang. Charcoal bands signify the nectar of the honey-ants; red-down bands, the red nectar-filled bodies of the storage ants; white-down rings, the acacia sugar; yellow-ochre bands, the yellow acacia blossoms.

At the conclusion of this honey-ant cycle, the young totemites lay down on the ground-painting and their bodies were rubbed in it. For, as the source of all honey-ant life, it was supposed to promote the increase of honey-ants and their ensured supply. (Photo by Professor T.G.H. Strehlow, © Mrs. T.G.H. Strehlow. Identified and documented by Mrs T.G.H. Strehlow from her husband's writings and his collection of 35 mm slides originally taken in Central Australia in 1955.)

'The Shaman knows that he is a spirit that seeks a greater Spirit. The great Spirit knows Death. Mother Earth knows Life. We were all born from the spirit and once we have lived, we will return to the Spirit. The Shaman knows that Death is the Changer. We do not eat live food. We kill our animals. If the seed or berry does not die when it is plucked, it will die in the teeth or the caustic juices of the stomach. All Shamans know that Death furnishes all with Life.'

These words of Hyemeyohsts Storm, medicine-man and *Heyoehkah*, convey the essence of the Native American practice of the Giveaway. In preparation for a Quest for Vision, the Sun Dance, or other occasions of holy prayer, the sweat lodge is entered, like a return to the womb, and gifts of prayer, herbs, fire, and water are offered to the Powers that guide and give life. The Lakota medicine-man Henry Crow Dog and his shaman son Leonard Crow Dog give away their prayers and purify themselves in the 'sweat' for 'all my relations' – that is, for the greater interdependent community of life. The photograph *above* is of a performer at the Sun Dance. His flesh has been pierced, and he gives his own heart-blood to the sun. (Sioux sweat lodge; Lakota sun dance. Photos by Richard Erdoes.)

Northwest Coast shamans' charms were created in order to aid wizards in curing or hunting. This particular Tlingit charm was found in the grave house of the Gunnah-ho clan on the Towtuck river between Yakutat and Dry Bay. The chthonic (earth) bear spirit devours one neophyte, while another waits under the paw of his slayer. The right hand of the man to be eaten touches the cheek of the wild beast. Eater and eaten are one. Thus life consumes life. Below them is a devil-fish spirit and above is the spirit of the whale. The whale, like the bear, for Northwest Coast peoples is associated with sacrifice and transformation. One belief is that the whale can swallow an entire canoe and pull it and all those aboard to the Undersea Village of the whales. To left and right of the central figure are sandhill cranes. (Ivory charm, ht $4\frac{3}{4}$ in., Tlingit, Northwest Coast, collected 1884–93.)

The slayer and the slain are in the field of a single impulse – that of self-sacrifice to a higher order of existence. The neophyte here affirms the covenant between the beast of the wilderness and himself by his delicate embrace of the representative of the feminine and absorbing aspect of nature. Flowing everywhere over the body of the chthonic tiger are serpents and felines, thunder, labyrinth, and spiral motifs. On the tiger's head stands a little deer, and on its back is a *t'ao-t'ieh* mask, symbolic of the destructive and perhaps even self-destructive forces at work in the universe. (Cast bronze Yu vessel, ht $13\frac{3}{4}$ in., Shang Dynasty, China, 1523–1027 BC.)

The jaguar for peoples of the Americas was a chthonic deity associated with shamanism and initiation. The neophyte-shaman is here being dismembered and devoured by a supernatural jaguar-initiator. The covenant between man and animal, the cooked and the raw, is once more demonstrated by the neophyte's hand on the jaguar's cheek. This gesture of affection seals the pact between eater and eaten. The enormous size of the jaguar in relation to the man puts the scene in the dream realm of ecstatic initiatory experience. From Texas to Patagonia, the jaguar is the shaman's familiar. In many cultures of the Americas, the shaman is capable of transforming himself into a jaguar. (Fired clay figurine, ht $4\frac{3}{4}$ in., Late Classic Maya, from Jaina Island, Campeche, Mexico, c. AD 800.)

In the Inunnit Eskimo stonecut, *right*, and in the contemporary Native American painting, *left*, an eagle carries a man to unearthly realms. Abduction to the Underworld by chthonic beings, or to the heavens in the talons of a predatory bird of initiation, is a key mythical theme common to many shamanic cultures. The image here portrays the Sun Bird as abductor. The eagle, symbolizing the Sun Father, or acting as his emissary, is the masculine initiator which fertilizes the feminine spirit, representing the sublime and dynamic relationship between the celestial principle and the forces of nature. The eagle, rising to great heights, overcomes the world and enters the gateway of immortality, the place of Origin. In many cultures, the eagle is depicted carrying a victim. This inevitably symbolizes the sacrifice of lower forces and the emergence of a higher order of existence. (Tempera by Jackson-Beardy, Island Lake, 1967; Stonecut print by Pudlio, Cape Dorset, Eskimo, 1963).

The Cuna people of the San Blas Islands believe that all things have souls. The world is full of good and evil spirits, called *Purbas*, who live in the eight levels of heaven and the Underworld. The *Purbas* can harm or cure an individual, depending on the situation. It is the shaman who is able to cajole, coax and outwit the demonic *Purba* if ill should befall someone. The winged feline depicted *below* holds a serpent in its mouth. Such demons can kidnap the soul of a man, woman or child and take it to one or another of the supernatural fortresses that are the lairs of these strange creatures. In the event of an abduction, the *nele*, or shaman, pursues the soul in his spirit canoe and does battle with the creature in order to retrieve the soul. (Applique, Cuna, San Blas Islands, Panama.)

Here the transformative nature of death is revealed in the image of the skeleton, holding the knife of sacrifice in its right hand and the deer antlers of rebirth in its left. The shaman's experience of death and rebirth, through a symbolic process of mortal self-wounding, is fulfilled in an experience of rebirth from the 'boneseed'. Deer and antlers are associated with the shaman's journey to the Other World. (Effigy vessel, Mixtec, Zaachila, Oaxaca, Mexico, c. AD 1400.)

The spirit that attacks and destroys the shaman-neophyte can become instructor, ally, and helper after the trials and ordeals of initiation have been endured. Among many Eskimo peoples, for example, the acquisition of spirits was often a violent process involving maiming and dismembering. The Eskimo shaman Niviatsian reported that, when he was being attacked by a walrus, two other spirits brutally ravaged him. This carving depicts a spirit wielding a knife of initiatory dismemberment. (Whalebone, antler, sinew, ivory, and stone carving by Karoo Ashevak, Spence Bay, Eskimo, 1972.)

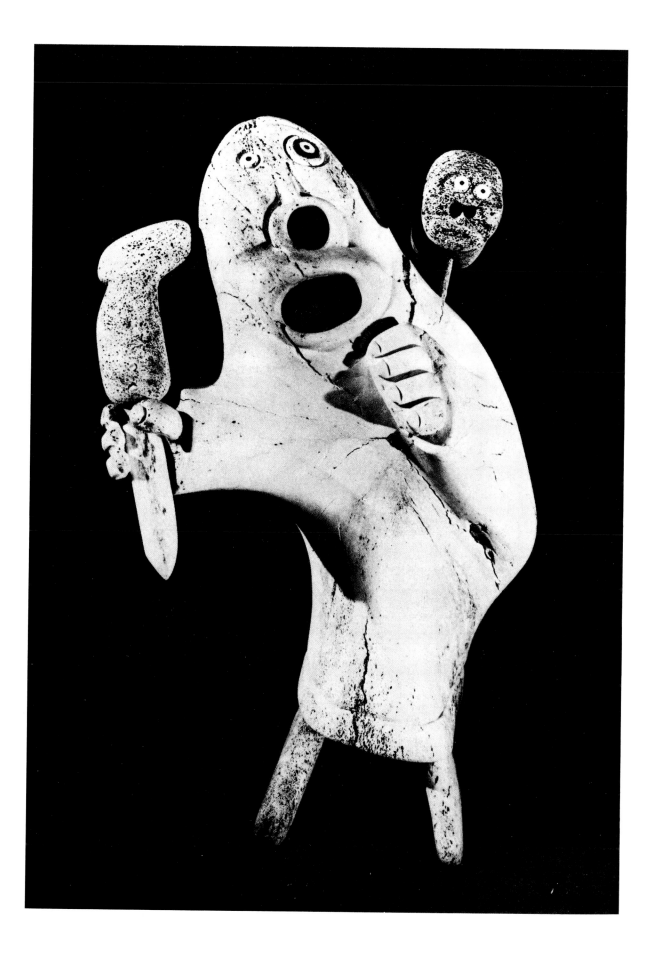

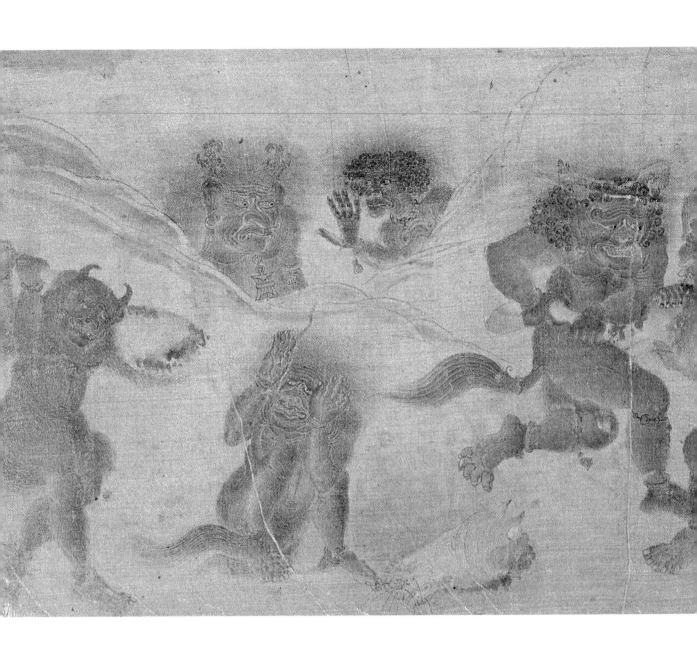

This Mongolian painting, influenced by Chinese art, depicts the malevolent power of demonic presences as they dismember a sacrificial horse. The horse, a mount for the dead among the Mongols, is often buried with the deceased. Perhaps this scene is a manifestation of the shaman's experience of self-wounding, an essential aspect of shamanic empowerment. The demons may represent the power of the secret forces of nature known to the Mongolian shaman who does battle for the deliverance of humans and beasts. The essence of the raw and untamed is released in the act of dismemberment. Through this representation of the symbolic act of dismembering life, one sees that symbolic death is the essential experience necessary to achieve shamanic vision, understanding, and power. (Painting by Mehmed Sikah Qalem, Turco-Mongolian, 14th c.)

Opposite:

This Eskimo shaman's drum from Nelson Island has a handle shaped as a shaman's body with entrails exposed and a kayak between the lungs. Inside the rim of the drum are worm-like figures that represent spirit helpers. In many shamanic cultures, the shaman's vital organs are removed and replaced with fresh new organs or quartz crystals. This supernatural surgery, one form of sacred dismemberment, allows the neophyte to be mortally wounded so that he or she can be reborn to a higher plane of being. This magic drum belonged in the last century to a woman shaman who employed it for weather forecasting, among other things. When the drum handle was put outside, the condition of its feet indicated what the weather would be. (Drum handle, wood, walrus stomach, human hair, animal teeth, fibre, red and black paint, Nelson Island, Lower Kuskokwim, Alaska, collected late 19th c.)

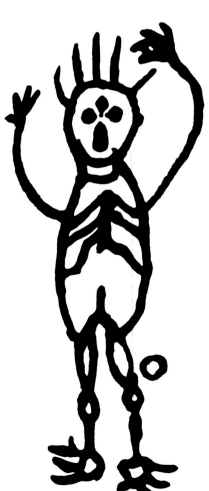

The Siberian Karagass shaman Tulayev's cap of green cloth is appliqued with a wolf's muzzle, with the moon above and stars on each side. All embroideries are made with the sacred white throat-hairs of the reindeer. Squirrel tails and feathers are attached to honour the shaman's animal allies. A ribbon, representing the shaman's spine and adorned with stars signifying heaven, hangs on the back of the cap. Bearing these symbols, the shaman is under the protection of heavenly spirits. His reindeer coat has strips of blue Chinese fabric on the front, symbolizing the breast-bone with ribs. On the back, embroidery portrays the spine and rib cage. Arm-bone applique appears on both sleeves. Wearing this unusual skeletal costume, the shaman who has already been dismembered by hostile spirits is protected against further attack. (Photo by Petri, c. 1927.)

Right:

In a shamanic world of cannibals, slaves, and journeys to the Underworld, the appearance of skeletonized figures is common. This radiant human figure is from the Northwest Coast culture region. (Drawing, after Wellmann, 1979, of rock painting from Monsell site, Salish, Nanaimo River, British Columbia.)

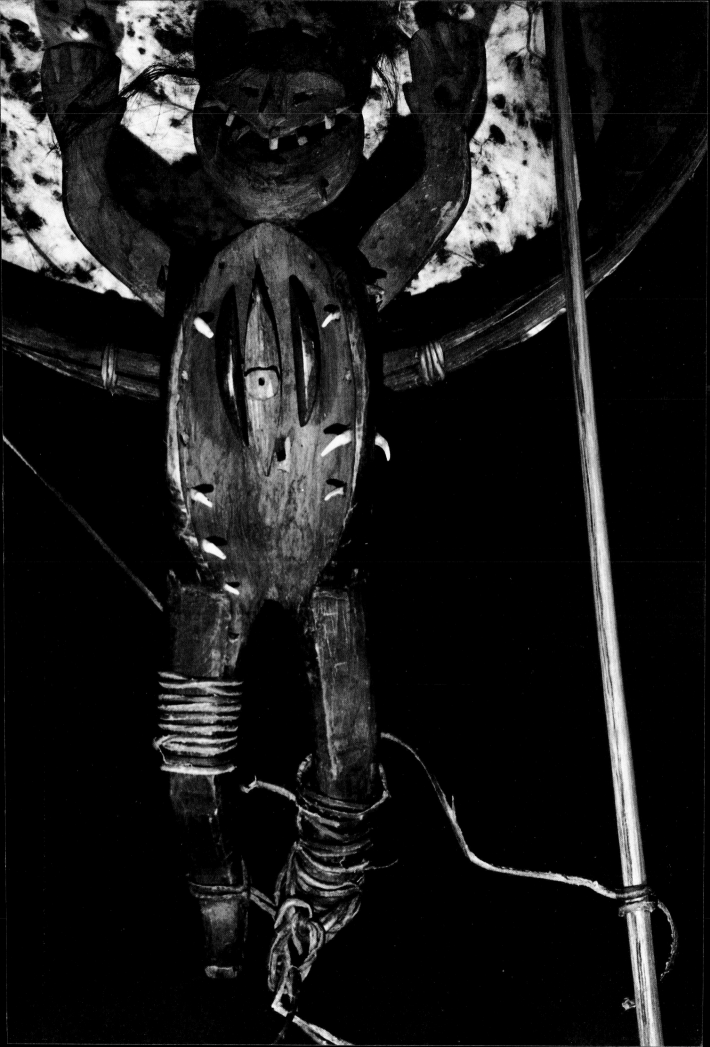

The Chumash of southern California particularly revered the sun. The most significant time of the year for these peoples was the winter solstice. The discovery of a certain cave in which the appearance of the solstice sun was recorded through a small opening is of extreme importance. In the cave are a series of paintings, one of which is illustrated here. The three figures depicted are associated with rain and water: the red-legged frog (left), the creature believed to be responsible for rivers and streams; the newt (centre), whose breeding cycle is associated with the rain following the solstice; and the common water strider (right). The shamanic solstice ritual included offerings of prayer and song to the sun in order to assure the cosmic balance so necessary to maintain life. (Drawing of rock painting, from Grant, *The Rock Paintings of the Chumash*.)

The rattle used by Northwest Coast shamans calls up energy from the depths, creating a sound field that awakens and unites. The carving or decoration on these instruments makes visible the world of supernatural beings and is the repository of their power as well. In effect, the rattle is the voice of the spirit when it is in use. Among Northwest Coast peoples, rattles were used to accompany singing, dances and oratory. They were carefully crafted in every detail, from the wood of the handle and body, to the grinding up of sacred pigments for colouring, and the type and number of seeds, crystals or stones used to create the sound. For the shaman, everything possesses power, and the bringing together of elements in the creation of a holy object or sacred musical instrument is one manifestation of the deep affinity the shaman feels for the natural and supernatural realms. (Sun-moon rattle, Northwest Coast.)

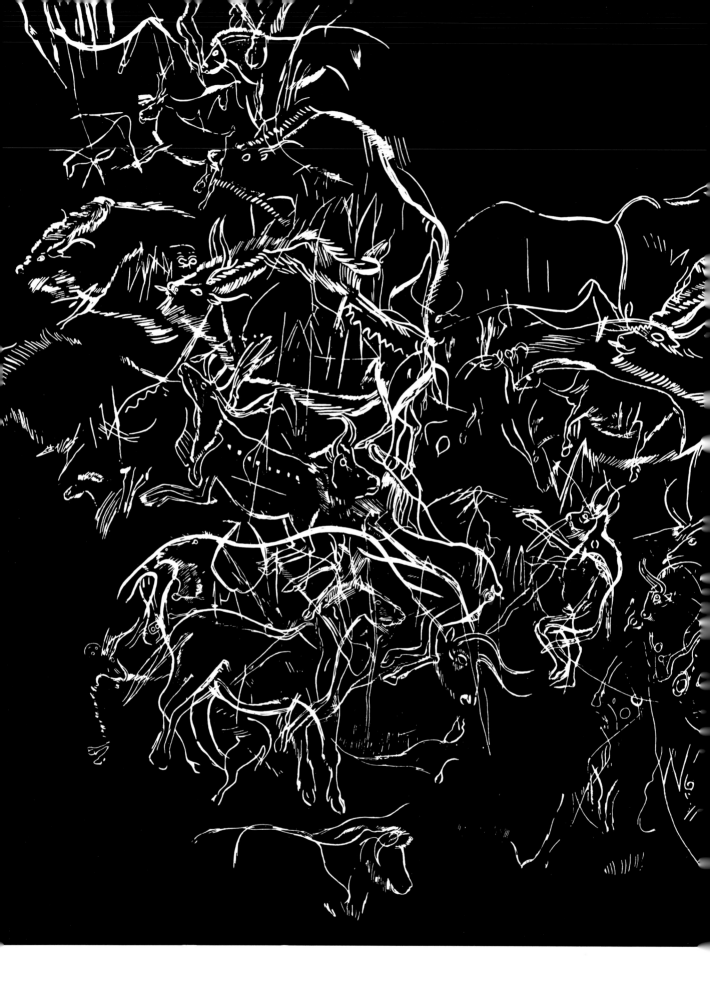

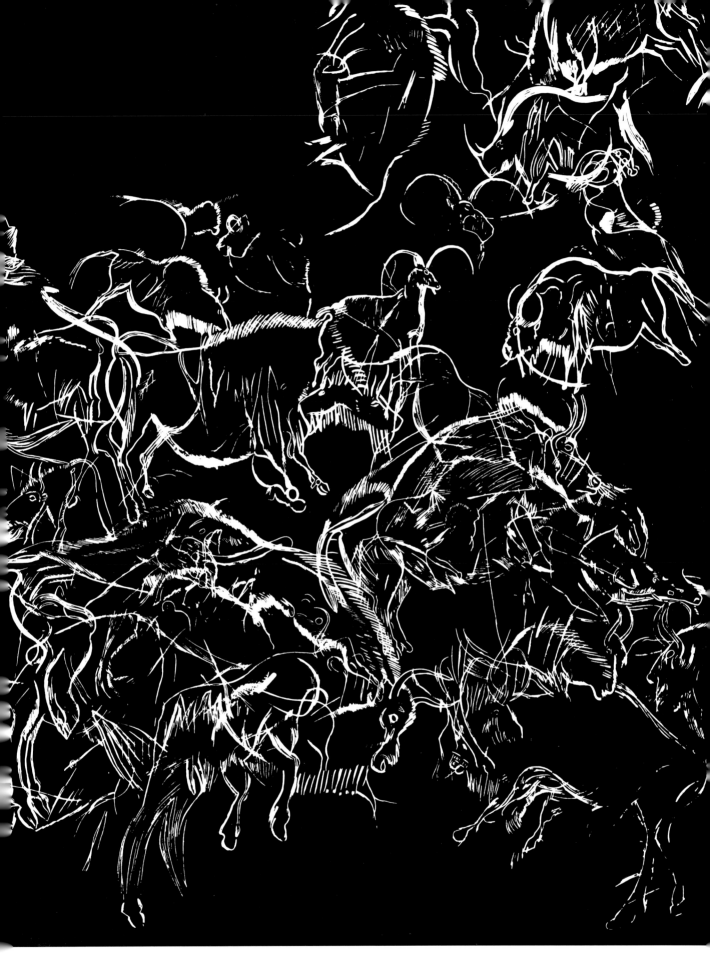

Caption overleaf

Above:
Lapp shamans were soothsayers at the court of Ivan the Terrible. Neighbours of the Lapps believed that the souls of these shamans could travel and report events from far away. The religious practices of the Lapps, including bear ceremonialism, indicate a strong relationship with Siberian peoples. A seventeenth-century European artist gives a view of the life of this shamanic culture: (1, 2) in the winter months, taxes of pelts and dried fish are paid to the king's commissioners; (3, 4, 5) travel is by reindeerdrawn sleds; (6) a reindeer may be eating the hallucinogenic mushroom *Amanita muscaria* as he is slain or sacrificed; (7) three men, one a shaman with his drum, drink an infusion, possibly of *Amanita*; (8) shaman and reindeer; (9) both collapse; (10) under the shaman's drum is the wizard in trance, while a spirit, part deer, part bird, officiates; (11) the shaman rises up from beneath his drum. ('The Manner of the Laplanders' Living in Winter', anonymous watercolour, 17th c.)

On previous page:
The tangle of beasts – bison, stag, horse and lion – that seem to dance on the wall of the Trois Frères cave in France could have been engraved to summon magically the creatures of the hunt. In the centre is a bison shaman playing a hunting bow. The bow, weapon of the earthly hunt, even today, is the caller of spirits among the Huichols, !Kung, Campa, and other shamanic peoples. It also functions as an instrument of conduction, first attracting the spirit, then moving it into the body of the shaman who is in trance. The bow thus bridges and unites earth and heaven, as it brings together spirit and matter. (Tracing by Henri Breuil after rock engraving, Les Trois Frères, Ariège, France, Magdalenian, Upper Palaeolithic.)

Right:

The use of *Amanita muscaria* was widespread among the Finno-Ugrian peoples of Siberia before the introduction of alcohol. The dancing shaman, a wizard from the Kamchatka district, sings and drums in a fierce trance state perhaps induced by the mushroom. The healing song of a Yukaghir shaman conveys the strength that characterizes Siberian shamanism:

> listen
> I'm a shaman
> spirits rise for me
> draw near me now
> animal spirits
> rise up now
> help me
>
> listen you
> invisible one
> my scream's a storm
> covering this world
> leave this man
> this sick one here
> leave this man
> alone

(Cloutier, *Spirit, Spirit*, 11.)

(Coloured engraving from *Moeurs et costumes de la Russie*, 19th c.)

On this rattle fragment two spirits sing, perhaps in response to a shaman's invocation. Song is the shaman's response to the power that has awakened within him or her. In essence, the shaman is being *sung*; so also, the shaman is *danced* by the powerful energies that he or she channels. Thus, art becomes a living expression of the visionary realm that awakens in wonder when death has been overcome. This vision song was sung to Lalalawrd-zemga when she was sick; she then used it to cure others:

In your throat is a living song
A living spirit song
His name is Long-Life-Maker
...
Yes I'm here to heal
With the healing ways
Of the Magic-of-the-Ground
And the Magic-of-the-Earth
...
So go on poor friend
And sing with the healing spirit
With the Magic-of-the-Ground
The Magic-of-the-Earth
...
And you will spring to life
Through the power of the words
Through the Magic-of-the-Ground
The Magic-of-the-Earth

(Cloutier, *Spirit, Spirit*, 77–8.)

(Rattle fragment, polychromed wood, Northwest Coast, collected late 19th c.)

This Tsimshian pole served as a ceremonial entrance to the house of Haidzermerhs. The great door hole represents the 'Hole through the Sky' through which the shaman passes in his sky journey. (Wooden pole carved by Hoesem-hliyawn, Tsimshian, Kitwancool, Skeena River, British Columbia, c. 1870.)

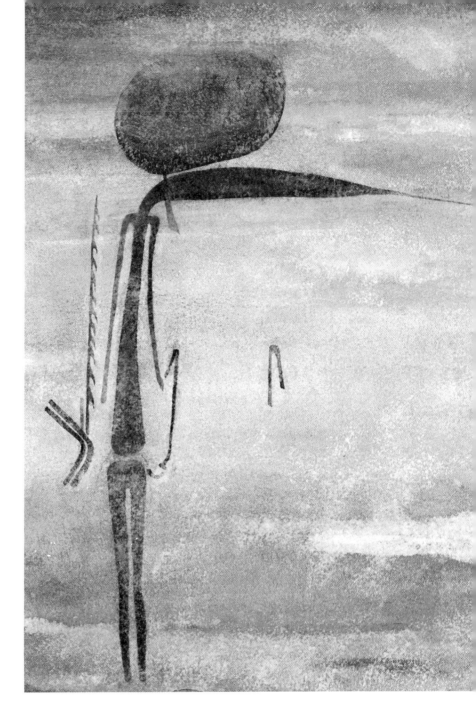

The sparsely inhabited Great Plains area of North America was the location of many different semi-sedentary peoples. At a late date, after the introduction of the horse by Europeans, a relatively homogeneous Plains culture emerged. The rock art of this enormous geographical territory reflects the diversity of its origins. The anthropomorphs depicted are radiant with power lines, and the interior of their bodies is depicted with geometric designs. Some of the fantastic man-like figures are antlered in the style of the shaman-dancer. Other figures appear to be spirit-birds, perhaps assistants to the medicine-man. The entire fresco gives the impression of flying or floating. (Pecked cave drawing, Wind River Indian Reservation, Upper Dinwoody Lakes, Wyoming.)

This ancient rock painting from Australia is a spirit figure, or more likely a shaman. In close proximity to the figure are the weapons of the earthly hunt – the spear and spear-thrower, boomerang and slingshot. The 'physical' head of the figure seems to be disappearing, and a great sun-like disc takes its place. This Dreamtime figure represents the often-seen magical relationship between the primitive hunt and the solar complex. (Drawing by Andreas Lommel of rock painting, Australia.)

In a mystical rapture, the Finno-Ugrian shamaness whirls as she flies, like a winged deer. Her trance may well have been induced by the sacred mushroom *Amanita muscaria*. Her garb is adorned with animal pelts, wings of predatory birds, and objects of fashioned metal. She herself has the appearance of an unworldly creature.

A Siberian Soyot song carries the essence of her ecstasy:

Shaman Drums
Oh! My many-coloured drum
[You who stand] in the forward
    corner!
Oh! My merry and painted drum,
[You who stand] here!
Let [your] shoulder and neck be
    strong.

Hark, oh hark my horse – [you]
    female maral deer!
Hark, oh hark my horse – [you] bear!
Hark, oh hark [you bear]!

Oh, [you] painted drum who [stand]
    in the forward corner!
My mounts – male and female
    maral deer.
Be silent sonorous drum,
Skin-covered drum,
Fulfill my wishes

Like flitting clouds, carry me
Through the lands of dusk
And below the leaden sky,
Sweep along like wind
Over the mountain peaks!

(Harner, *Hallucinogens and Shamanism*, 51.)

(Photo by Kurt and Margot Lubinsky.)

Opposite below:
The Eskimo wizard is borne through the night sky on a magical sled by a spirit-goose. The grey goose of the Arctic is a valued bird and appears in the myths, songs, and images of many Eskimo peoples. It is a creature of physical and spiritual sustenance. Like the wild gander of European mythology, the goose is at home in the water, on land, and in the air. It has mastered the three realms of existence, and thus is identified as the shaman's spirit-helper. ('In the Night Sky', stonecut print by Mary Pitseolak, Cape Dorset, Eskimo, 20th c.)

The Taoist saint and shaman Li Tieh-kuai, the Immortal, was reputed to be able to leave his body at will and fly to the heavens in order to converse with Master Laotse. On one of his celestial adventures, he returned to earth and, unable to find his own body, slipped into the body of a crippled beggar who had just died. He wandered about the countryside on crutches in his new body, and occasionally would send his spirit to heaven to continue his discourses with his Otherworldly master. The ability to fly, converse with the dead, and 'manage' another body than his natal body is common to shamans in many areas of the world. (Painting on silk by Yen Hui, China, 13th c.)

A masked and antlered shaman holds an ear of young corn and a planting stick as he stares through the ages from a canyon wall in southeast Utah. Although no date is known for this compelling figure, the wizard's antlers point to a hunting culture, the corn to an agricultural – and thus more recent – culture. Many Native American societies that still practise the art of shamanism have retained features that characterize a much earlier subsistence type and social structure. As shamans have traditionally been the repositories of the culture's sacred and secular traditions, both early and recent, they often embrace in their communication style and attire the most relevant historical and contemporary elements of those traditions. (Screen print after a canyon painting, S.E. Utah.)

An oracular mirror from China, on the Siberian shaman's right shoulder, assists him in seeing the worlds beyond and in capturing lost souls of the dead. Hanging everywhere on his tunic are images of helping spirits. On the back he wears the symbolic bones of his own resurrection. The bells on the costume tell the shaman certain things he needs to know. The plaits, pendants and ribbons sewn to the costume are called 'tails' and 'wings', indicating the shaman's ability to fly. Other motifs that appear on the typical Siberian shaman's tunic are the rainbow, the World Tree, the Sun Door, and well defined bones and organs. (Shaman's costume, Tungus, Siberia, late 18th c.)

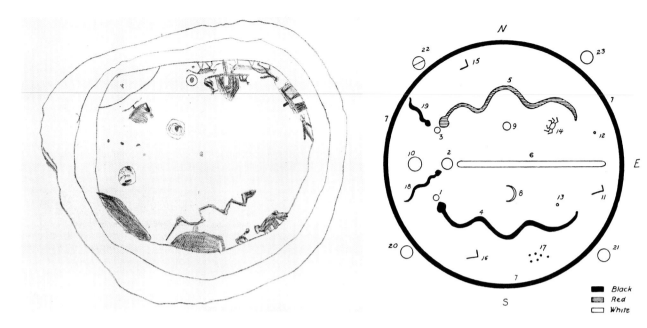

Maps

Shamans transmit to their people in sign, song and dance the nature of the cosmic geography that has been revealed to them in the process of initiatory trances and soul journeys. Map-makers and myth-dancers, shamans live internally in a multidimensional realm continuous with so-called ordinary reality. Most of the maps depicted in this section, although briefly described, are exceedingly complex and sophisticated.

The three worlds of the Siberian Chukchee are represented by concentric circles. The innermost embraces the ordinary world. In the centre is the Polar Star, and on the left are stars, Sun and Moon, the latter holding a lasso with two human captives; beneath him is the black mountain of darkness. A *kelet* (spirit) earth house is at the bottom. Two *kelet* walk on all fours, and a large, stinging worm wriggles above the house. The Left-hand Dawn has a low house with two murderers tied to it. The house of the Genuine Dawn is on a platform supported by a pole. Four dogs are tied to the sides. Dawn-Top-Woman lives in the region of the Right-hand Dawn (see upper left), in a little house supported by a single pole. Venus is under her feet. (Drawing, collected by Waldemar Bogoras, from Bogoras, *The Chukchee.*)

The Diegueños of Southern California convey the design of their world in the ground-painting that is done during the boys' puberty ritual. The circle is the horizon. The broad white line is the Milky Way. (1, 2, 3) mortar and pestle used to grind up the hallucinogenic Jimson weed; (4, 5) rattlesnake; (6) Milky Way; (7) world's edge; (8) new moon; (9) full moon; (10) sun; (11) coyote; (12) buzzard star; (13) crow; (14) black spider; (15) wolf; (16) Orion, mountain sheep; (17) Pleiades; (18) black snake; (19) gopher snake; (20–23) mountains. (Drawing after ground-painting, Diegueño, S. California.)

This Chukchee drawing represents the path of a shaman who is being led around by Mushroom Men in the Other World. These spirits are related to the ritual ingestion of the hallucinogen mushroom *Amanita muscaria*. The shaman at first thinks he is a reindeer, then he is 'submerged' (in a shamanic trance). The Mushroom Men are said to live in a separate realm, and are very powerful beings despite their small size. (Drawing collected by Waldemar Bogoras, from Bogoras, *The Chukchee.*)

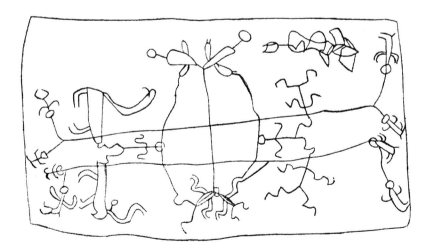

The Lapp shaman's drum is map and territory. The following figures are painted on the drumhead: (1) Hora-galles, thunder god, with hammers to drive away evil spirits; (2) Veralden-olmai, Man-of-the-World, with thorns to symbolize abundance; (3) Wind-Old-Man, who dwells on a shaded forest branch whence he sets the wind blowing; (4) shaman of heaven; (5) Ruta, disease god; (6–8) sacrificial black hen, reindeer bull, sheep; (9) two lines separating heaven from earth; (10–12) festival men; (13) sun; (14) 'domest-icated' road with church, house, cow and goat; (15) sacrificial horse; (16) Underworld shaman; (17) Underworld with church and house; (18–20) Juksakka, Sarakka, Madderakka; (21) sea with fish, a reminder of the means of travel in the Underworld; (22) Lapp village; (23) Leibolmai; (24) bear. (From Gray, *Mythology of All Races*, IV.)

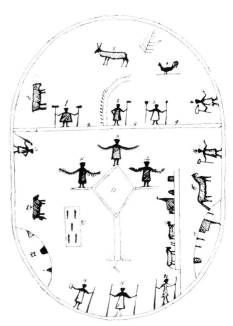

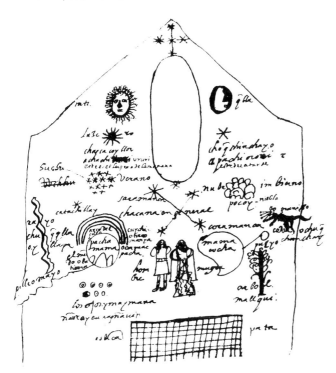

This Inca cosmogram, according to anthropologist Douglas Sharon, depicts diurnal, seasonal, and stellar rhythms of nature, with their positive and negative effects 'on the interdependent network of life shared on this earth by human beings, plants and animals'. The design, from the back wall, above the main altar of the Temple of the Sun in Cuzco, Peru, was copied by the native chronicler Juan de Santacruz Pachacuti-Yamqui. Above, we have Orion's Baldric, sun, moon, morning and evening star, and Viracocha. In the middle, we find lightning, summer clouds, winter fog, hail, and coca cat; the Southern Cross, with corn pot and coca pot, Pacha Mama and rainbow on the left and Mother Sea on the right. Pilcomayo, Lord Earth, Pleiades, Man, Woman, and Tree are above the cross-hatched altar. (From M. Jiménez de la Espada, *Tres Relaciones de Antigüedades Peruanas*, 1879.)

The *mesa* or altar of power objects used by the Peruvian shaman, Eduardo Calderón Palomino, reflects the elements of the Inca cosmology *above*. The tripartite zoning represents a synthesis of masculine and feminine, procreation and regeneration. In front is a can with the juice of the hallucinogenic San Pedro cactus. To the left is a stalk of San Pedro.

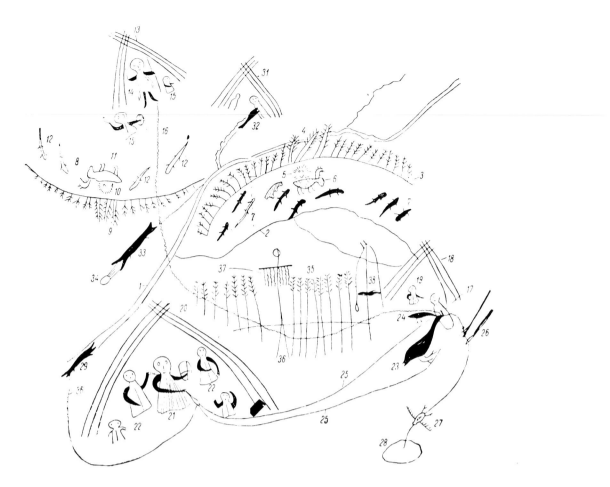

Paths to the Underworld

In some shamanic cultures, the path of initiation is an invisible one. Scrolls, labyrinths, meandering trails, and straight lines, all roads of varying meaning, denote the 'orientation' of the neophyte's direction. Certain forms, such as the labyrinth, represent explicitly the experience of initiation – entry into the abyss of the mysteries, the pilgrimage of the spirit. The journey is in fact an expression of the evolution of the human spirit out of worldly time and space.

This extraordinary Siberian cartoon depicts the manner in which the shaman of the Nyurumnal clan sent disease to the Momol clan. Another part of the drawing shows a shamanistic healing seance. The drawing is carefully numbered and each element is elaborated as follows:

(1) Podkamennaya Tunguska River;
(2) its tributaries;
(3) lands of the Momol clan;
(4) the clan's sacred tree;
(5) mistress of clan territory;
(6) patron spirit of the clan;
(7) spirit watchmen;
(8) land of the Nyurumnal clan;
(9) place of their clan cult;
(10) Nyurumnal clan's mistress spirit;
(11) patron spirit of the clan territory;
(12) spirit watchmen of the clan;
(13) shaman tent of the Nyurumnal;
(14–15) Nyurumnal shaman and his assistants;
(16) track of the shaman spirit sent by the Nyurumnal shaman to destroy the Momol clan;
(17) the destructive spirit penetrates the Momol blockade of spirit-watchmen, changes into a wood-boring worm, enters the entrails of a Momol clansman and begins to destroy him;
(18) the sick man's tent;
(19) his wife;
(20) Momol shaman tent;
(21) shaman divines cause of illness;
(22) clansmen attending the shaman's ritual;
(23) shaman's spirit-goose;
(24) shaman's spirit-snipe; goose and snipe put their beaks into the patient's entrails to catch the disease spirit;
(25) tracks of shaman's spirits;
(26) disease-spirit leaps out but is caught by the spirit-helpers; the splintered pole holds the spirit while the knife stands guard;
(27) shaman orders his owl-spirit ally to swallow the disease-spirit and carry it to the anal opening of the Lower World;
(28) entrance to the Lower World;
(29–31) shaman then sends his ally, the two-headed pike, to take vengeance on the Nyurumnal;
(32) pike tears out victim's 'corporeal soul';
(33) soul abducted by pike-spirit;
(34) 'corporeal soul';
(35) Momol shaman builds fence of larch-spirits where alien spirit penetrated;
(36) watchmen (splintered poles) placed over alien spirit's track;
(37) pelts of sacrificed animals hung there;
(38) reindeer skin sacrificed to the supreme deities.
(Drawing after A.F. Anisimov.)

'When you shamanize,' exclaimed a Siberian shaman, 'you find your way, by yourself!' Desiring to be a shaman, an Eskimo once went to a great wizard and said, 'I come to you because I desire to see.' The wizard looked into his eyes and turned toward the great white emptiness of the endless snowscape: 'Your direction can be found . . . there. . . .' The approach to this infinite mystery is made alone. For only in the solitudes do the spirits that destroy and teach appear. The potency of the journey, and the relationship between birth, death, and sex, is evidenced by the prominent penis on the figure *above*. The figure *below* holds something in his hand, perhaps a stalk of corn. Below it appears to be a basket. The figure has bird feet and an antlered head, a motif common to shamanism the world over. The left arm continues into a precise rectangular scroll design. Another symbol for the path is the scroll which, like the labyrinth, contains at its centre a protected sanctuary of the mysteries. (Drawings, after Wellmann, 1979, of rock carvings, Inkom, Idaho (above) and Little Colorado River region, Arizona, Late Pueblo Style III – Early Pueblo Style IV.)

Below left:
This drawing by a Barasana, of the Vaupés territory of Columbia, represents the way to the Other World, the territory that is revealed after the ingestion of the plant hallucinogen *Banisteropsis caapi*. The partakers of these visionary plants say that the 'horizon opens like a door'. Thus the entry is made to the realm of spirits. (Drawing, after Reichel-Dolmatoff, *The Shaman and the Jaguar*.)

Below right:
The Siberian Chukchee, according to anthropologist Waldemar Bogoras, believe that the dead journey to an Underworld guarded by wild dogs who attack those who have been cruel to dogs during their lifetime. Kin of newcomers guide them on their way. This sketch was drawn by a Chukchee after a deep swoon where he saw the many roads that lead to the Afterlife Place. The entry holes are in varying sizes. The smallest are intended for those who died by strangulation. Not only do the dead journey to this realm, so also do shamans in their trances. (Drawing from Bogoras, *The Chukchee*.)

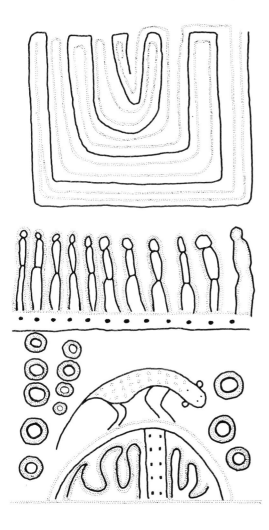

Thresholds of the Two-light World

According to a Siberian shaman, 'As I looked round, I noticed a hole in the earth. . . . The hole became larger and larger. We (shaman and spirit ally) descended through it and arrived at a river with two streams flowing in opposite directions.' (Popov, 138.) The two directions of the journey, one pointing to the temporal and the other to the atemporal, meet at the cosmic centre. The 'opening' between realms is frequently represented as a hole, like the birthgate, that is the threshold between womb and consciousness. The Mexican Huichols call this gate or passageway *Nieríka* (see below). The Chinese representation of this concept is of heaven, *Pi*, a jade disc with a hole in the middle. This concept is also encoded into ritual: thus, the Pomo of Northern California strike the initiate with a bear paw. The blow is supposed to make a hole in the initiate's back which causes death and subsequent rebirth. Natural orifices are equivalent rebirth portals – the fontanel, the navel, the vagina, and the anus. The concentric circle and spiral motif are the most common type of this ubiquitous form.

This Apache medicine skin, or prayer chart, owned by Hashke Nilnte, was considered to be extremely powerful. The three large figures are gods in their abodes: Sun Boy (on the left), giver of morning light and healing; Creator of All (centre); and First Goddess. Above and left of the Creator is the nucleus of the universe, Night Girl, who was a spot in which a form appeared at the beginning of time, to emerge as the Creator. The four quadrated discs are each four mythological personages: on the left makers of dreams and visions, and on the right sky and earth messengers. Sun and moon flank the central figure, who is haloed and associated with lightning.

Four gods are at the corners. All the round figures resemble the Huichol *Nieríka*. (Painted hide, photo by E.S. Curtis, from *The North American Indian*, I, 1907.)

In a ground-painting made by Australian Aborigines, tracks of the mythical emu surrounded the birthplace of the ancestor Karora, from which all life, and the sun itself, emanated, and into which Karora passes at the end of his life. The shaman enters this place in the process of his initiation. (Ground-painting, photo from the Mountford Sheard Collection of Ethnology, State Library of South Australia.)

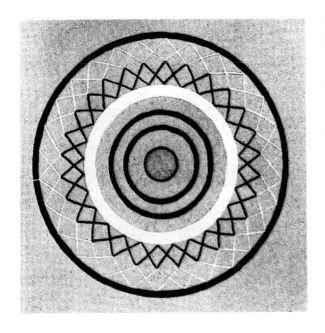

The Southern California Luiseño sand-painting figure depicts the 'place of emergence' of the Ancient Ones and the 'Navel of the Universe', indicating the relationship that exists between the Earth Mother and her people. The painting, done during a funeral ceremony, is the door to the Other World. The simple, abstract design is made with white ash and coal dust, both of which are symbolic of fire or life that has gone out of existence. (Drawing of sand-painting and interpretation by David Villaseñor, 1963.)

The Huichols have made the *Nieríka* or prayer offering into a sacred art form. The word *Nieríka* means also the 'face' of the deity; a mirror; and the threshold through which one passes into the transpersonal realms. Here the five sacred directions, the sacred four cardinals and infinite centre, intersected by the intercardinals, are depicted in the field of purifying fire. The absolute centre point is the gateway to the infinite field of the divine. (Yarn picture, Huichol, Mexico. Author's collection.)

At the climax of a peyote ceremony, a celebrant left the sacred ritual to enter the night of his visions. The clear night sky shone with stars as he danced alone – a hunter seeking the sacred deer. Another worshipper too departed from the circle of chanters and entered the darkness. The two encountered each other in a wide meadow, and she found herself being lifted onto the shoulders of the young man. As he danced with her, she felt herself transformed into a slain deer. At the moment of her symbolic death and release, a great *Nieríka* appeared to the slayer and the slain. Together, they became one spirit as they travelled through the portal of vision. (Painting by the deer-dancer, Michael Brown (Rising Eagle), USA, 20th c. Author's collection.)

Departure and incubation

The departure from the light world of ordinary waking consciousness to the inner psychological regions associated with suffering and death takes many forms. Spontaneous ecstasy, dreams, crying for a vision, abduction by a demon-monster, incorporation by a chthonic deity, sickness, madness, formal trials and ordeals, all direct the shaman-neophyte's attention toward a cosmos that is but barely revealed to the ordinary individual. At the turn of this last century, for example, the Arctic explorer, Knud Rasmussen, inquired of an Eskimo acquaintance if he was a shaman. The man responded that he had never been ill nor had dreams; therefore, he was not an *angakok*. Hungry spirits and ingenious sacred practices devour the shaman's fear, preparing the Holy One for his or her vocation.

Among the Chukchee, spirits (*kelet*) are divided into three classes: (1) evil, invisible spirits that bring disease and death, (2) bloodthirsty cannibals that fight against the Chukchee warriors, and (3) spirit helpers of the shamans. The *kelet* depicted here are cannibals who have stolen an infant's soul from its father and are about to eat it. (Drawing collected by Waldemar Bogoras, from Bogoras, *The Chukchee*.)

This wooden mask from Sri Lanka depicts Maha-kola-sanni-yaksaya, the great demon of fatal disease, and his eighteen servant demons, or *yakku*. Every *yakku* has a particular place where he lies in wait for his victims, and can also send illness over a long distance. The term for demon-sickness is *tani-kama*, which means 'aloneness' or 'separateness'. The curing ceremonies conducted by shaman trance-mediums are addressed to all eighteen *yakku* in turn, with a different mask for each. At the end of the ceremony the patient is taken to a deserted place and left for dead, to deceive the demons. (Poly-chrome carved wood, Staatliches Museum für Völkerkunde, Munich.)

The Japanese Buddhist shaman, the *yamabushi*, participates in a ceremony known as the *nyūbu* or *mineiri*, which is an initiatory ritual of fasting, mountain ascent, purification, and rebirth. The process itself has been called *taini-shugyō*, or 'exercise within the womb'. On Mount Omine, at the place of Nishi-no-nozoki, is the precipice over which each member of the ceremonial party is dangled. With hands clasped over the head, the *yamabushi* is required to confess, a symbolic penance of hell and purification. (Photo by Inoue Hiromichi.)

15 西の覗きに罪障を懺悔

An Eskimo shaman spirit, with leg bones and inner organs revealed, seems to stalk his prey with sacrificial blade in hand. The *en face* deer mask reveals the transcendental nature of the spirit's bloody mission. (Stonecut print by William Noah, Barnabas Oosuaq and Martha Noah, Baker Lake, Eskimo, 1970. Sanavik Cooperative, Baker Lake, on loan to the Winnipeg Art Gallery.)

The theme of incorporation by an undersea monster is familiar in many cultures. Here, the shaman-neophyte is being consumed by a shark. (Sculpted effigy, Colima, Mexico, c. AD 100. Private collection.)

73

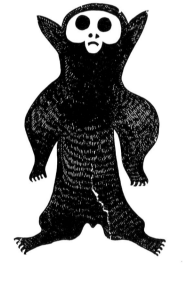

Spirits of the Underworld

The relationship of the shaman with the spirit realm is complex and varied. In some cultures, one class of spirits is regarded as evil, another class is believed to be helpful. In other cultures, the spirits that dismember the shaman ultimately become allies. Some spirits tutor; others obstruct. The acquisition of spirits for most shamans is essential to the effective practice of this art. Spirits can possess the shaman or sing, as ally, in the near proximity. Each culture, and in some instances, each shaman, has a particular relationship with this world of the unseen. The spirits pictured *above right, left and below,* however, all have the role of frightening or symbolically destroying the shaman-neophyte.

Above left:
The helping spirit, Issitoq, assists in locating those who have breached taboos. Known as Giant-Eye, his melancholy nature and peculiar appearance was portrayed by the Eskimo Arnaqaoq. Shortly after Arnaqaoq had lost his parents, Issitoq appeared to him and said, 'You need have no fear of me; I too struggle with sad thoughts, therefore I will follow you and be your helping spirit.' (Drawing by Arnaqaoq from Rasmussen, *Rasmussens Thulefahrt.*)

A variety of startling spirits of European and Arctic origin. (Drawing of a demon figure from El Ratón de Hoz de Guadiana; 'The Big Lemming', stonecut print by Pudlo, Cape Dorset, Eskimo, 1961; Carving of a *tupilak* (spirit), Eskimo, collected in Angmagssalik, E. Greenland, 1931–2. National Museum of Denmark, Department of Ethnography.)

A gigantic and ominous spirit bird appears in a dream forewarning the dreamer of a coming blizzard. The mystical quality that Tudlik conveys in his stonecut print is one reflection of the impulse among many Eskimo artists to be in a living relationship to the spirit world of the past. (Stonecut print by Tudlik, Cape Dorset, Eskimo, 20th c. Dorset Fine Arts, Ontario.)

Death and skeletonization

The skeletonized shaman figure is the personification of death. At the same time, like the seed of the fruit after the flesh has rotted away, his or her bones represent the potential for rebirth. The shaman-neophyte must die to finitude in order to attain knowledge of the immortal. The sacred dismemberment of the shaman's body is a manifestation of the realm of chaotic multiplicity. The shaman is reborn from his or her boneseed to a higher order of existence.

A Buryat shaman wears a tunic appliqued with ribs and sternum. Siberian shamans often wear this sign of their initiation. (American Museum of Natural History, New York.)

X-ray style, with inner organs and skeletal structures depicted, is seen in shamanic art, from the cave paintings of Palaeolithic France to the modern Huichol yarn pictures. The rock figure from Oregon is one of many examples in the Northwest where shamanism is still practised today. This particular figure has a rayed head and on its right concentric circles, perhaps representing the entry to the Other World. (Drawing after Wellmann, 1979, from rock carving, Long Narrows Style, now in the Winquatt Museum, The Dalles, Oregon.)

According to religious investigator Juan Negrín, this Huichol image conveys 'the physical distintegration and material mutation that accompany the apotheosis of the spiritual essence of Watakame (the First Man), who becomes a permanent energy for effective cultivation of maize and squash'. Watakame survived a great flood with the help of Our Great Grandmother Growth. Under her direction, he laid the foundation for human life on earth. Upon his death, the various parts of his body were scattered and transformed into new plant life. (Yarn picture by José Benítez Sánchez, Mexico, c. 1972–80. Collection of and photo by Juan Negrín.)

Opposite, above left:
Skeletonized shaman archer. (Drawing by William Noah (b. 1943), Baker Lake, Eskimo, 1970. Mr and Mrs K.J. Butler, Winnipeg, on loan to The Winnipeg Art Gallery.)

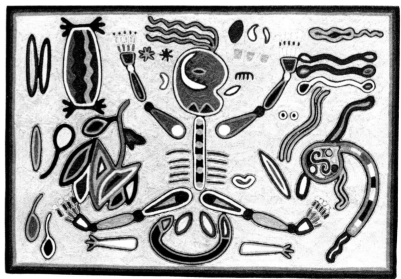

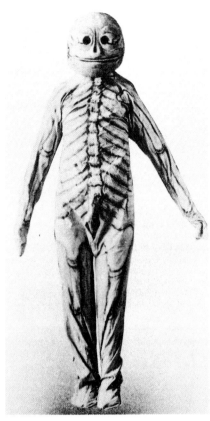

Tibetan Buddhism is profoundly influenced by the ancient shamanistic religion of Bon-po. By AD 630, with the advent of Buddhism, the theatre of shamanism was incorporated into Buddhist practice. This *Atsara*, or death figure, appears in many of the theatricals. One account describes the character as follows: 'As a rule, three or four *Atsara* wth their tight-fitting, one-piece garb, on which skeletons are painted, dash first into the arena to perform a terpsichorean extravaganza, pirouetting, leaping, hopping, bending their bodies backwards and forward, waving their arms, and turning somersaults, or relapsing into a solemn movement as a slow ballet step accompanied by mystical and rhythmical motions of hands and fingers.' Elsewhere the *Atsara* are described as ghouls who chase the pilfering Raven with long sticks. The image of death in life, of life consuming life, is fundamental to the Vajrayana tradition. (From Laufer, *Oriental Theatricals*.)

Like the shaman, dancing on the threshold of the dual unity, this figure, *right*, half skeletonized, half fleshed, is a manifestation of the conjunction of opposites. (Ceramic figure, Tlatilco, Mexico, 1700–1300 BC. Regional Anthropological and Historical Museum, Villahermosa, Tabasco, Mexico.)

This ancient Chinese bowl has on its interior a skeletonized figure. The bowl's T-pattern, a precursor of ideographs, may have imparted supernatural powers. (Pottery bowl, Yan-shao, China, c. 2200–1700 BC. Museum of Far Eastern Antiquities, Stockholm.)

Covenants and animal transformation

The communion between culture and nature occurs first in the realm of spirit. The shaman has died to the phenomenal world, the world of everyday reality. The ravenous spirits of the Underworld have dismembered and consumed the neophyte, thus releasing him or her to a higher order of existence where the cooked and the raw become one. In a state of surrender, the initiate is receptive to the teachings from the spirit world. Bear, frog, raven, eland, seal, wolf, and mosquito instruct through the very act of destruction – a covenant forged in death *and* in spirit between the eater and the eaten.

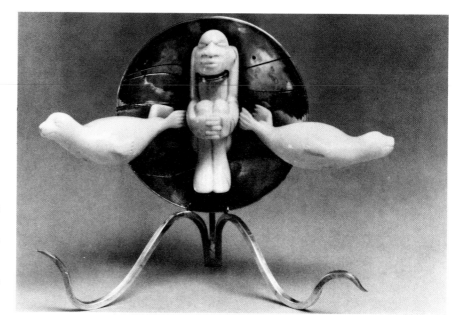

An Eskimo shaman carved of seal ivory sits in trance as his animal nature takes over. The figure seems to be whistling the song of the seal as he undergoes the transformation process. The Eskimo artist Lawrence Ahvakana, who crafted this mystical sculpture of ivory and sterling silver, explains:

'For a lot of people their second person is an animal. I have a second person. I think it's a seal or an owl. And I use these animals a lot within my sculpture pieces, and I try to make it realistic. It's not a fairy tale that I'm going through. It's real, because I've felt it many times and I've felt it while I'm hunting. So I am trying to understand more of myself, I guess, and just trying to understand what my surroundings are, what influences me, when I work.' (Sculpture by Lawrence Ahvakana (b. 1946), Eskimo, 1975. Visual Arts Center of Alaska, Anchorage.)

An Eskimo is surrounded by five blood-sucking mosquitoes. One bites his neck, another his lower back, and a third the tender back of his knee. All three points of penetration are areas of great vulnerability. The exaggerated size of the insects indicates that this is a dream.

The 'little' mosquito has more power than the man. The dreamer looks at something. The object is not identified, but perhaps it will function to arrest the irritation of the one who is dreaming. This engraving conveys one way in which knowledge is transmitted between creatures and culture. ('Mosquito dream', stonecut print by Kalvak, Eskimo, 1965. Reproduced by permission of the Holman Eskimo Cooperative, Holman Island, Northwest Territories, Canada.)

A rainbow transects the bodies of eight figures with antelope heads and human legs. Perhaps a group of !Kung shamans are in the process of transforming themselves from man to creature. At the left end of the rainbow is an *ales*, a winged antelope that appears in rock paintings in which the theme of transformation is found. (Drawing after Pager, *Ndedema*.)

A Northwest Coast Tlingit Raven rattle; the most significant of the creatures of nature for Northwest Coast peoples is the raven. Full of supernatural power, Raven is Trickster, Transformer, culture hero, and Big Man – the world creator. Raven's ability to transform himself is unparalleled; he can change himself into anything at will. He can fly to the sky realm, descend to the ocean's depths, or fly to the farthest reaches of the earth. A mad Trickster, Raven frequently finds himself the butt of his own mischief. The hawk on the breast of the raven (i.e. on the belly of the rattle) is also a powerful supernatural being, sometimes representing Thunderbird, sometimes not. And for many peoples, the frog symbolizes resurrection and fertility. Its amphibious quality represents the transition from water to earth, and points to its lunar aspect, its periodic appearance and disappearance in relation to the seasons of the year. The potential of rebirth then is the essential transmission between frog and shaman, the knowledge of the pairs of opposites. (Raven rattle, polychromed wood, Tlingit, Northwest Coast, USA.)

The bear spirit instructs the shaman in the way of animal wisdom. Animal tutors prepare the shaman-neophyte for the journey to the untamed realms that he or she must enter on behalf of others. The smoking of sacred tobacco by Native American people was done as a prayer offering to the guiding spirits of the universe. (Redstone pipe bowl, East Dakota. Lindenmuseum, Stuttgart.)

Life energy force and the ally of power

In the quest for power, the shaman seeks experiences with animals, geographical sites, and unusual weather conditions. Many shamans, particularly from the Americas, associate this power with their ally, the serpent, guardian of springs and representative of the forces of nature. Ania Teillard has described the serpent as 'An animal endowed with magnetic force. Because it sheds its skin, it symbolizes resurrection. Because of its sinuous movement, it signifies strength. Because of its viciousness, it represents the evil side of nature.' It is a potent manifestation of the energy of birth and rebirth, sex, and death. All *mysteries* of the universe, like the great sun and moon, the cycle of the seasons, and the sounds of dawn, are regarded as a manifestation of unseen power. Behind and feeding this power is an ever greater power – Sila of the Eskimos, Wakan of the Sioux. There are few cultures that have endeavoured to represent the greater power, but many have depicted this life energy force that activates body and soul-essence.

The !Kung of South Africa have a concept of 'energy' called *N/um*, a 'supernatural potency' that makes healing possible. The trance-dancer's activation of *N/um* is associated with shamanic powers, including healing, clairvoyance, X-ray vision, prophecy, and soul travels. The heat of the dance and the fire boils the 'medicine' up the spine and out of the hands and head. In this state, the healer can use the *N/um* 'to pull out' the sickness of others. The !Kung refer to *N/um* as 'a death thing', so powerful are its effects. The younger trancers frequently are unable to control the 'medicine' and find themselves in chaotic states. More experienced healers then have to 'draw off' the energy and calm the frenzy. The figure *above*, a rock painting from the Ndedema Gorge, South Africa, depicts a newly slain antelope with rays of energy emanating from the belly and heart. The antelope was an extremely important animal to the !Kung. It was a beast that provided them with physical and spiritual nourishment. *On the left* is a badly damaged fragment of a rock painting from the same area. Two antelope shamans appear to have *N/um* streaming from the crowns of their heads. (From Pager, *Ndedema*.)

2

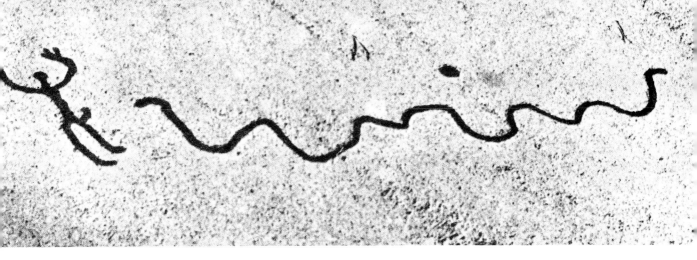

The Scandinavian god Thor, known as Defender of the World, has his origins in the Palaeolithic world of the hunt. This shaman hero figure has attributes of the Trickster. Here an ithyphallic figure raises his hammer against a serpent with seven curves. This image could well represent Thor's battle with the Midgard monster serpent. (Rock carving, Bohuslan, Sweden.)

In central California, shamans, in whose dreams the rattlesnake appears, lure the venomous creatures out of their dens in the spring and 'work' the serpents in rites of healing and protection. The Hopi, on the other hand, believe their Sky God to be a horned and plumed serpent. The spiral serpent, with its relationship to the moon and water, denotes wisdom and great energy, the primogenic and cosmic forces in a constantly evolving cosmos. (Rock carving of spiral horned serpent, Fremont Style, Nine Mile Canyon, Utah.)

The Mexican Huichols believe that all things are infused with varying degrees of life energy force, *kupuri*. Shamans have great *kupuri*. So also does peyote, the hallucinogenic spineless cactus that is their sacrament. From each peyote plant streams radiant flower-like *kupuri*. Around each is a glowing field of energy. The eaters of this holy plant come to know this radiance, this vitality. (Yarn picture by Prem Das, Huichol, Mexico. Author's collection.)

Equilibrium and compassion

The stag, reindeer, and deer, the medium of magical transport for the shaman, is believed to be a mediator between heaven and earth and a messenger of the gods. The antlers, symbolic of regeneration and growth because of the way they are renewed, are often associated with the Sacred Tree and the mysteries of death and rebirth. Antler symbolism goes back to the Palaeolithic of France, and the Mesolithic and Neolithic of Europe and Asia. Symbolic images of cervids and human skeletons with antler crowns are found in England, France, Persia, Asia Minor, and China. The association of the cervid with the heavenly sun and the light of dawn is found in Asia. The ancient Scythians, for example, referred to the 'golden animal proceeding through the air, spreading light.' Many shamanic peoples recognize this creature as having great mystical gifts, beauty, sensitivity, grace, and compassion. A source of physical as well as spiritual sustenance, the deer is identified by the Huichols of Mexico and Hopi of the Southwest with rain and abundance. The Huichols associate the deer with their holy sacrament, peyote, which gives them vision and heart. And, finally, the deer is healer and shaman, finder of supernatural plants, and singer of the songs of the gods. The tension of pairs of opposites is resolved in the figure of this creature.

The 'Dancing Sorcerer' of the Magdalenian cave Les Trois Frères in central France is a composite of many different creatures. His head is crowned with reindeer antlers, his ears are those of the wolf, and his face is bearded like a lion's. He has a horse's tail and bear paws. The startling eyes seem to pierce through the thousands of years since this image was rendered. (Drawing, after Breuil, of cave painting, Les Trois Frères, Ariège, France, Palaeolithic.)

A Siberian Tungus shaman with antlered head sings, dances and drums in his village. The engraving was done in 1705 by Nicolas Witsen, a Dutch diplomat at the Tsar's court. (Engraving from *Noord en Oost Tartarye*, Holland, 1705.)

This anthropomorphic figure was excavated from the tombs at Ch'an-sha, Hunan Province. Human figures with stag horns generally represent shamans who have received superhuman authority from the gods; the extruded tongue has been associated with prayers for rain, the teaching of wisdom, or communication with the supernatural realms. (Wood and antler sculpture, China, 4th c. BC. British Museum, London.)

This deer mask figure is from the Mississippian Southern Cult, Spiro Mound. (Carved cedar wood mask with shell inlay, Oklahoma, c. AD 1200. Museum of the American Indian, Heye Foundation, New York.)

This is a Huichol depiction of Tatewari, Our Grandfather Fire, the first shaman. In the centre Tatewari is depicted with *kupuri*, or life energy force, flowing from the sides of his antlered head. A radiant projection of *kupuri* arises at the fontanel, between the pairs of opposites represented by his antlers. On his right is the feminine life-giving corn in the red masculine field of fire. On his left is the venomous masculine scorpion in the blue field of the feminine waters of life. Two offering bowls with energy streaming between are at the top of the picture. In the lower area, a *takwatsi* (medicine basket) is depicted. This is woven in the design of the rattler's skin, and on top of it is repeated the antler motif. (Yarn picture, Huichol, Mexico. Author's collection.)

Masked Mongol holy man, seen on an Imperial Progress through Central Asia by Tsar Nicholas II (1868–1918).

World Tree and *Axis Mundi*

The Centre of the World, the *Axis Mundi* or world axis, the 'unmoved mover' of Aristotle, is the threshold place between space and spacelessness, between multiplicity and unity, between mortality and immortality. It is said of this cosmic centre that it is everywhere. And yet peoples of all times and places have found and created finite representations; even the 'solarized' shaman with nimbus is a manifestation of this. Eliade has noted that the peak of the 'Cosmic Mountain' is not only the highest point on earth, but the earth's navel, the origin of creation. The Cosmic Mountain allows the seer a vantage point of all-seeing; and its ascent is associated with loftiness of spirit. The World Tree, like the Cosmic Mountain, is the point of contact between heaven and earth. Tree and mountain both intersect the three realms of existence: the Underworld is penetrated by the roots of the Tree and is in the belly of the Mountain; the Middle World is transected by both; and the crown of the World Tree and summit of the Holy Mountain are both received by the heavenly realm.

The most numerous and spiritually powerful shamans in Korea are female possession trancers, called *mudang*. The shaman ritually constructs a model cosmos in which the human and nonhuman beings relevant to a crisis are brought together in harmony. Guiding spirits grant her power to mediate the personal, social, and cosmic healing process. The *mudang* serves as mediatrix for the human, nature, and spirit communities which inhabit the three cosmic zones. She has a special rapport with the spirits of mountains, which are sacred centres and cosmic portals. She may also construct a symbolic World Axis at the site of her ritual. In the photograph, a 68-year-old *mudang* dances for more than an hour upon parallel-bonded knife blades atop a platform in the centre of her court-yard, which is both a model cosmos and the residence of her guiding spirit, Taegam. This ritual (*kut*) honours Taegam, deity of the home, earth-site, wealth, and blessings. The *mudang* ascends to the Sky Realm, overcomes the vulnerability of flesh through sacred power and supreme balance, and returns to the Middle World to communicate messages from the spirits. (Korean shamaness, Seoul, Republic of Korea, 1977. Photo by Edward R. Canda.)

Among the Evenks of Siberia, a birch tree is placed at the centre of the shaman's ceremonial tent, enabling the shaman to descend to the Underworld or ascend to the Heavenly Realm. Animal familiars and spirit helpers attend the shamanic seance. (From A.F. Anisimov, *Sbornik museja antropologii i etnografii*, XII (1949).)

The use of the sacred mushroom, fly agaric (*Amanita muscaria*), was brought to the Americas by Siberian peoples long ago. Its use among present-day native peoples of Middle America is doubtful. This miniature depicts a shaman seated beneath what seems to be a fly agaric. Perhaps he is healing. There may have been another figure in front of him. The mushroom itself suggests a tree, as *Axis Mundi*. (Clay sculpture, Nayarit, Mexico, c. AD 100.)

A female *machi* (shaman) has ascended her *rewe* or notched pole. The pole has steps, and the *machi* climbs to the seventh level to complete her skyward journey. She plays a frame drum that assists her in her climb up the World Tree. In the Mapuche region of Chile, the hallucinogens *Anadenathera*, *Datura*, and *Brugmancia* were used during shamanic seances. (Photo by Louis C. Faron.)

On the Third Sacred Day of the Lakota Sun Dance, the Sun Pole is erected. A bundle of sweet grass, sage, and buffalo hair is placed in the fork of the pole. Songs are sung to mark this powerful moment:

> At the centre of the Earth
> Stand looking around you.
> Recognizing the tribe
> Stand looking around you.

(Photo by Eugene Beuchel, Rosebud, 1928.)

An Australian Aboriginal Fire Ceremony. (From Spencer and Gillen, *The Arunta*.)

Flight

The shaman's association with bird figures is found the world over. The bird always denotes rising, activation, change, and vitality. In some traditions, the bird is symbolic of the soul; in others the bird is recognized as an intelligent collaborator with man, the bird being the bearer of celestial messages.

A procession of antelope shamans with antelope heads and hoofed feet march across a wall of Procession Shelter in the Ndedema Gorge, South Africa. This powerful !Kung fresco includes an *ales*, a delicate flying antelope related to the

mysteries of transformation. The flying deer is part of the mythology of such diverse cultures as the Samoyeds of Siberia and the Huichols of Mexico, and is associated with magical flight, trans-figuration, and spiritualization. (From Pager, *Ndedema*.)

These two Eskimo ivory geese were found in the grave of a shaman with other carvings and remnants of human bones. The geese were part of a shaman's medicine kit. The goose is frequently associated with the mystic journey to the Other World. Further-more, shaman and waterbird were essentially analogous, as both were masters of the three realms of existence.

These two lovely carvings were perhaps spirit helpers that assisted the shaman in his or her magical journey. (Ivory carvings, Dorset culture, from Mansel Island, Northwest Territories, Canada, c. AD 500. National Museum of Man, Ottawa; J-10180-22.)

A birdlike shaman spreads his wings and opens the fan of his tail in a mystical dance of flight. Atop the head appear antlers or rays – a sign of great power. To his left is an open hand – a corporeal sign of his inner state. The raised hand symbolizes the voice in song, strength and power. (Drawing by Wellmann, 1979, of rock carving, Blackbird Hill, Nebraska.)

This Eskimo Oonark drawing depicts the wizard in flight accompanied by his animal familiars or spirit helpers. Caption: 'When the moon rocket went to the moon and some of the young kids were trying to tell the old people about this, they were getting really frustrated because the old people were saying, "Oh, that's nothing, my uncle went to the moon lots of times".' (Drawing by Jessie Oonark (b. 1906), Eskimo, 1971. Winnipeg Art Gallery; acquired with funds donated by Imperial Oil Ltd.)

Opposite, below right:
The magical emu featherwork woven into these Australian sandals disguised the tracks of the sorcerer (*kurdaitcha*), who wore them to cast spells on an enemy encampment or carry out a blood vendetta. According to one account, the sight of the distinctive tracks of the spell-maker's sandals could literally frighten an enemy to death. (Feather sandals, West Australia, collected 1927. Field Museum of Natural History, Chicago.)

Right:
An Eskimo shaman with the aid of the drum prepares himself for his spirit flight. His body is bound up as he begins his magical aerial journey. The most proficient Eskimo shamans are reported to be able to fly around the earth, to the moon, and into deepest space. (From Rasmussen, *Eskimo Folk Tales.*)

Turning away from everyday life and turning inward ultimately opens the shaman to the infinite cosmos. The move away from the world takes the shaman-neophyte through the wound-door to a realm of terror and sacrifice, decay and death. Destruction thus becomes instruction as the shaman surrenders to the untamed forces of nature. The Haida grave-figure is a commemorative effigy of a deceased shaman as his disincarnate soul, transformed into a crane, travels to far-off realms. (Carved wood figure, Haida, Northwest Coast. American Museum of Natural History, New York.)

Mastery of fire

The shaman's mastery of fire is related to the mastery of ecstasy. The contact with conditions of excessive cold or extreme heat indicates that the shaman has gone beyond the ordinary human condition and is now a participant in the sacred world. The rousing of mystical heat in order to achieve fire-mastery is common to mystics and shamans the world over. The ability to withstand the rigours of a winter waterfall or the heat of burning embers is a manifestation of great power and a symbol of biological and spiritual maturation.

The *Velada* (night vigil) is an ancient Mazatec (Mexico) healing ceremony conducted by a shaman who has ingested sacred hallucinogenic mushrooms. Mushrooms are also given to the patient and those participating in the seance. The shamaness, María Sabina, pictured here, raises her hands in prayer and supplication. She chants:

> Woman of the Southern Cross am I.
> Woman of the first star am I.
> Woman of the Star of God am I.
> For I go up into the sky.
> . . . . .
> Woman who stops the world am I.
> Legendary woman who cures am I.

(Wasson, *The Wonderous Mushroom*, 17–207.)

The mushrooms 'speak' through the shaman, illuminating the condition of the patient. (Photo by A.B. Richardson.)

A Japanese *yamabushi* (Buddhist shaman) in the ritual of *saito-goma* demonstrates his mastery of fire. The *saito-goma* is an ancient Buddhist fire ritual originating in pre-Buddhist shamanism. Fire, symbolic of life, allied with the concept of control and superiority, is a representation of an agent of transmutation. It is a medium into which forms vanish and from which they are born. It purifies or destroys that which is evil. (Uji Temple ritual. Photo by Fosco Maraini.)

'It is one, it is a unity, it is ourselves.' These words were spoken by Huichol shaman, Ramón Medina Silva, when he described to anthropologist Barbara Myerhoff the purpose of the peyote ceremony. This yarn picture depicts a sacred assembly of *peyoteros*, peyote eaters, who celebrate 'their life' throughout the night. At the top of the circle, the shaman, or *mara'akame* officiates, seated on his *uweni* (shaman's chair). The unifying circle connects the celebrants who chant around a five-plumed fire, the ancient Grandfather shaman. The holy event transpires in a field of radiant and purifying fire. (Yarn picture, Huichol, Mexico. Author's collection.)

Every year, small groups of dedicated Huichols travel several hundred miles by foot and public transportation to their Paradise, Wirikuta, the Sacred Land of Peyote. Upon their return to their villages in the Sierras, they are greeted by their families and friends in celebration. Here women and children hold up lit candles as offerings of thanksgiving to the gods who have guided the pilgrims safely home. The delicate, illumined candle, an offering of light and fire, is, like the lamp, symbolic of individuated light, or the life of the individual.

The Native American medicine-man's portable altar is his pipe, a mystic symbol of the union of nature and culture which is seen here being offered to the Sun. In the words of the Lakota medicine-man Lame Deer: 'For us Indians there is just the pipe, the earth we sit on and the open sky. . . . That smoke from the peace pipe, it goes straight up to the spirit world. But this is a two-way thing. Power flows down to us through that smoke, through the pipe stem. You feel that power as you hold your pipe; it moves from the pipe right into your body. It makes your hair stand up. That pipe is not just a thing; it is alive.' (Lame Deer and Erdoes, *Lame Deer: Seeker of Visions*. Photo by Richard Erdoes.)

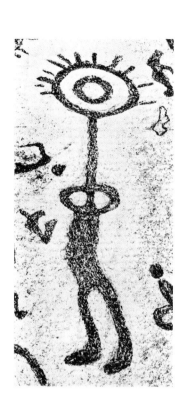

Solarization

The nimbus or halo emanating from the heads of these shamans and spirits is a visual expression of intellectual energy in its mystical aspect, or of supernatural power. The sun itself is symbolic of the heroic principle of all-seeing and all-knowing, and the indwelling fire of life. The activation of this 'internal sun' we have called 'solarization'. It represents the highest spiritual manifestation of totality. The halo seen in old high culture religions is a relic of earlier solar cults.

This Algonkian sun figure could be a spirit or a shaman. Gordon Wasson has made the important discovery that the hallucinogen fly agaric was in sacred use by the peoples of this area. (Rock carving, Peterborough, Ontario.)

This Sioux chief is wearing a feathered headdress like an aureole. Like the unconquerable Sun, *Sol Invictus*, the Plains warrior draws the blood of his victim and gives his own blood for the salvation of 'all his relations'. (Detail from painted buffalo hide, Sioux. Musée de l'Homme, Paris.)

Shaman, hero, Trickster, the god Thor, is shown with a halo of fire around his head. The heat of his presence was so tremendous that he was not permitted to cross the Rainbow Bridge. His thunderbolt hammer fashioned by dwarfs, his magic belt that doubled his strength, and his glove of iron that allowed him to handle his red-hot hammer, all added to his lustre as warrior and saviour. (Engraved stone slab, Niederdollendorf, Rhineland, Frankish, 7th c. Rheinisches Landesmuseum, Bonn.)

An extraordinary rock art figure from Northwest Australia features a detailed and rayed aureole enhanced by wavy lines of energy. The figure is a totemic ancestor that emerged from the depths of the earth at the beginning of the Dreamtime and returned to these chthonic realms at the end of the Dreamtime journey. (From Grey, *Journals of Two Expeditions of Discovery*, I.)

The rich remains of an ancient culture, preserved by the desert climate of the Southwestern USA, are attributed by the modern Pueblo peoples to the 'Anasazi', old ones or ancestors. The solarized figure here, with rayed head, symbolizes the great power of those who have received the spirit of light. (Rock painting, Anasazi culture, Petrified Forest National Park, Arizona.)

A Huichol *Nieríka* depicts the radiant, androgynous spirit of the hallucinogenic peyote, a source of *kupuri* or life energy. The heart area is prominent; when you ask a Huichol why they eat peyote, the answer is often 'Because it gives you heart.' To right and left are censers with burning copal, five-starred peyote buttons, and candles. In front of the spirit is an eight-tufted peyote button – perhaps representing the cardinal and intercardinal directions. (Yarn picture, Huichol, Mexico. Author's collection.)

Return to the Middle World

The true attainment of the shaman's vocation as healer, seer, and visionary comes about through the experience of self-wounding, death, and rebirth. Knowing intimately and personally the realm of sickness, decrepitude, dying and death readies the shaman for his or her actual mission. The shaman has a social rather than personal reason for entering these realms of suffering. For the Work is directed toward the healing of person and society in relation to the greater cosmos. The shaman, however, is not only a wounded healer; he or she has effected a process of self-healing as well, and is thus an example of one who has the ability to transform self, others, and nature. By dying in life, the shaman passes through the gates of fire to the realm of eternally awakened consciousness. Having tasted immortality, the laughter of compassion wells up from the human heart. The suffering that the shaman endures, then, gives rise to the realm of play, for the shaman is both in *and* out of the field of life. The faces of many shamans are riven with suffering and lined with laughter. The Trickster, the Wise Fool, emerges to dance the forces of nature, to sing the songs of creatures, to dream the way of the future.

Opposite:
The North American Lakota medicine-
man, Henry Crow Dog, emerges from
the sweat lodge after offering prayers to
the Great Spirit. (Photo by Richard
Erdoes.)

The Waiká shaman, of the Venezuelan
Upper Orinoco, here dances and sings
as his soul travels to the spirit world. His
song may well be directed to spirits
called *Hēkurā,* with whom he is
communicating. (Photo by the mission-
ary Luigi Cocco of Indio Yanoama of
Upper Orinoco, from Biocca, *Yanoama:
The Story of a Woman Abducted by
Brazilian Indians,* London 1969.)

Above:
A Ladakh shamaness in trance prays
during a mediumistic seance. She
throws sacred rice into the air as an
offering. This particular healer-medium
travels from house to house to work
with the sick and ailing. (Photo by
Robert Gardner.)

Return to the Middle World

Shamans, medicine people, seers, and visionaries still practise the arts of healing and trance in various parts of the world. Many, in their different ways, are endeavouring to pass on the wisdom of the Ancient Ones to the people of today. They know that the traditions of the past are threatened by modern technology. But, as one shaman said to this author, 'Many non-traditional people of the West seem not only to appreciate the "road" of the shaman, but also appear to have an affinity for the "Medicine Way".' The return to the Middle World of today, then, involves a bridging of culture and time. As we have seen, shamans are trained in the art of equilibrium, in moving with poise and surety on the threshold of the opposites, in creating cosmos out of chaos. The Middle World, then, is still a dream that can be shaped by the dreamer.

Opposite:
Pete Catches (Petaga Yuha Mani, He Walks with Coals of Fire), a Lakota medicine-man, lives his profound vision as he gives himself to the Sun during the powerful Sun Dance. He was called to his vocation by the Thunder Beings. (Photo by Richard Erdoes.)

A Siberian shaman, at the turn of the century, plays his frame drum during a healing ceremony that takes place in a family dwelling. (American Museum of Natural History, New York.)

Below:
In front of his offering (*inau*) of willow shavings hung on wands, an Ainu of Northern Japan prays to the *kami* or spirits that inhabit the unseen world.

Sources

Alcheringo. Ethnopoetics, vol. 1, Boston (Mass.), 1975

Anisimov, A. F., 'The Shaman's Tent of the Eveuks and the Origin of the Shamanistic Rite', in Henry N. Michael (ed.), *Studies in Siberian Shamanism*, Toronto, 1963.

Blackburn, T. C. (ed.), *December's Child*, Berkeley, London, 1975.

Boas, F., *Kwakiutl Ethnography*, Chicago, London, 1966.

Bogoras, W., *The Chuckchee* (American Museum of Natural History Memoirs, vol. 11), Leiden, New York, 1904–9.

Boyd, D., *Rolling Thunder*, New York, 1974.

Cloutier, D., *Spirit, Spirit*, Providence, 1973.

Cooper, J. M., *The Gros Ventres of Montana (Part II)*, Washington DC, 1957.

Curtis, E. S., *The North American Indian*, Cambridge (Mass.), 1907–30.

Eliade, M., *Shamanism*, New York, London, 1964.

Eliot, A., *Myths*, New York, 1976.

Elkin, A. P., *Aboriginal Men of High Degree*, New York, 1977.

Furst, P. T., 'Huichol Conception of the Soul', *Folklore Americas*, vol. 27, no. 2 (June 1967).

Grant, C., *Rock Art of the American Indian*, Golden, 1980.

——, *The Rock Paintings of the Chumash*, Berkeley, Los Angeles, 1965.

Gray, L. H. (ed.), *Mythology of All Races*, vol. 4, New York, 1964.

Grey, G., *Journals of Two Expeditions of Discovery in North West and Western Australia*, vol. 1, London, 1841.

Halifax, J., *Shamanic Voices*, New York, 1979, Harmondsworth, 1980.

Harner, M. J. (ed.), *Hallucinogens and Shamanism*, New York, 1973.

Holmberg, U., *Mythology of All Races*, vol. 4, New York, 1964.

Ivanov, S. I., *Materiali po izobrazitel' nomu iskusstvu narodov Sibiri XIX nacala XX v.*, Leningrad, 1954.

Lame Deer and R. Erdoes, *Lame Deer*, New York, 1972, London, 1973.

Laski, V., *Seeking Life*, Austin, 1959.

Laufer, B., *Oriental Theatricals*, Chicago, 1923.

Legeza, L., *Tao Magic*, London, New York, 1975.

Lévi-Strauss, C., 'The Effectiveness of Symbolism', *Structural Anthropology*, New York, London, 1963.

Lommel, A., *Shamanism*, New York, 1967.

Myerhoff, B. G., *Peyote Hunt*, Ithaca, London, 1974.

Neihardt, J. G., *Black Elk Speaks*, Lincoln (Neb.), 1961, London, 1972.

Ortiz, A., 'Look to the Mountaintops', in E. G. Ward (ed.), *Essays on Reflection*, Boston (Mass.), 1973.

Pager, H., *Ndedema*, Akad. Druck- und Verlagsanstalt, Graz, 1971.

Perry, J. W., *The Far Side of Madness*, Englewood Cliffs, 1974.

Philippi, D. L., *Songs of Gods, Songs of Humans*, Princeton, 1979.

Popov, A. A., 'How Sereptie Djarroskin of the Nganasans (Tavgi Samoyeds) Became a Shaman', in V. Dioszegi (ed.), *Popular Beliefs and Folklore Tradition in Siberia*, Bloomington,1968.

Rasmussen, K., *Across Arctic America*, New York, 1968.

——, *Eskimo Folk Tales*, London, 1921.

——, *Intellectual Culture of the Hudson Bay Eskimos*, Copenhagen, 1930.

——, *Intellectual Culture of the Iglulik Eskimos*, New York, 1976.

——, *The Netsilik Eskimos*, New York, 1976.

——, *Rasmussen's Thulefahrt*, Frankfurt a/M, 1926.

Reichel-Dolmatoff, G., *The Shaman and the Jaguar*, Philadelphia, 1975.

Sharon, D., *Wizard of the Four Winds*, New York, London, 1978.

Spencer, B., and F. Gillen, *The Arunta*, New York (forthcoming).

Teillard, A., *Il Symbolismo dei sogni*, Milan, 1951, quoted in J. E. Cirlot, *A Dictionary of Symbols*, London, 1951.

Wasson, R. G., *The Wonderous Mushroom*, New York, 1980.

Wellmann, K. F., *A Survey of North American Rock Art*, Akad. Druck- und Verlagsanstalt, Graz, 1979.

Acknowledgments

Objects reproduced in the plates, pp. 33–64, are in the collections of the author 45; Mr and Mrs K. J. Butler 34; Göttingen, University Collection, Museum für Völkerkunde 64; Istanbul, Topkapi Saray Museum 48–9; Kyoto, Chion-Yi Monastery, Japan 63; London, British Library (Ms Add 5253) 56–7; Mexico, National Museum of Anthropology 43 below, 46; Munich, Staatliche Museum für Völkerkunde 50 above, 61; New York, American Museum of Natural History 33, 42, 58; Ottawa, National Museum of Man (72–8261) 38; Paris, Cernuschi Museum 43 above; Mrs F. C. Reif 53; Sitka, Sheldon Jackson Museum, Alaska 51; Winnipeg, Hudson's Bay Company 44 above.

Photographic sources:
PLATES Akademische Druck- und Verlagsanstalt, Graz 60–1; Nicholas Bouvier, Cologny-Genève 57; Robert Braunmüller, Munich 64; Peter T. Furst 43 below, 46; New York, Association on American Indian Affairs 47; Eberhard Otto 59; Ottawa, National Museums of Canada 38; Indian and Northern Affairs 44 above; Winnipeg Art Gallery (Ernest Mayer) 34.
THEMES American Federation of Arts, New York 78 above; American Museum of Natural History, New York 85 below; Canadian Eskimo Arts Council, Ottawa 78 below; Claes Claesson 81 above; Peter T. Furst 73 below, 84 below; D. Mazonowicz 65; Harold Moore 85 above r.; National Museums of Canada, Ottawa 86 above r.; J. M. Pelt, *Drogues et plantes magiques* (Paris 1971) 89 above; Dr. D. Sharon 67 below; Gorai Shigeru, *Yama no Shukyo* (Kyoto 1970) 73 above r.; Romas Vastokas 90 above l.; Robert Gordon Wasson, Harvard Botanical Museum, Cambridge (Mass.), photo A. B. Richardson 88 above l.; K. F. Wellmann (see Sources) 81 below l., 91 below l.; Peter Young 81 below r.